# You
# Are a
# Magnet

# You Are a Magnet

## Guiding Principles for a Magnetic and Joyful Life

AMBER LYON

First published in Great Britain in 2024 by Hodder Catalyst
An imprint of Hodder & Stoughton Limited
An Hachette UK company

The authorised representative in the EEA is Hachette Ireland, 8 Castlecourt
Centre, Dublin 15, D15 XTP3, Ireland (email: info@hbgi.ie)

3

A CIP catalogue record for this title is available
from the British Library

Hardback ISBN 9781399725743
ebook ISBN 9781399725750

Typeset in Helvetica by Goldust Design

Printed and bound in Great Britain by Clays Ltd, Elcograf S.p.A.

Hodder & Stoughton policy is to use papers that are natural,
renewable and recyclable products and made from wood
grown in sustainable forests. The logging and manufacturing
processes are expected to conform to the environmental
regulations of the country of origin.

Hodder & Stoughton Limited
Carmelite House
50 Victoria Embankment
London EC4Y 0DZ

www.hoddercatalyst.co.uk

To whoever picked up this book
ready to see things in a new way.

# Contents

# An Invitation to Change

Change is an elusive concept. We tie it to time, place and our physical appearance, but so rarely do we acknowledge the meaningful change that's triggered from within. The type that is so small, yet mighty that it ripples through every aspect of our lives. Deeper relationships, rewarding careers, a kinder internal world – they all begin with a single choice to see things differently.

Over the years, as a magnetic-mindset coach, I've worked with hundreds of clients from different countries, religions, beliefs and backgrounds, all of whom have done the work and felt their inner and outer worlds begin to glow in a new way. To do what they have done, all that's required is you and your willingness to see things in a new light. By choosing this book, you have begun to awaken your innate personal power and magnetism. Now is the perfect moment to take responsibility for your life and all its potential.

With each of the essays in these pages, you will be invited to shift your perspective and lean into the guiding principle that carries you closer to love, rather than reinforcing fear. I encourage you to earmark those that resonate deeply, so that you can return to them, while intuitively allowing yourself to spend more or less time on each one, depending on what you need in the moment. Let yourself be guided by the experience of truth as you read, signalled by an inner nod of recognition, rather than a need to intellectualise. And when you've read it all, keep it close and return to it, as it will gift to you what you need in each moment. Consider each of the guiding principles as a hand to hold as you venture towards your own inner truth. Thank you for opening your mind and your heart to these essays; I hope they serve you as they have me and those that I work with.

# Welcome

I've felt called to write this book for as long as I can remember. Something quiet, deep inside of me, longed to share the lessons I have learned throughout my life in the hope of helping others. In every meditation and still moment with myself, the message was clear: share your words with the world. But I felt like this dream was too large for my life, and always found an endless list of reasons why I simply couldn't rise to the challenge. I tried to justify, reason and prove my fear-based mindset till I was blue in the face. I sought out odd jobs, got led down other paths and chased ideas of what I thought I *should* be doing. I ran towards careers and outward validation to try to outpace the quiet inner knowing that there was a greater calling for me to follow. It's something we are all familiar with – *pretending not to know ourselves as well as we really do*; hiding from ourselves by trying to be someone else and ignoring the light within us that holds the answers we seek. Eventually, I realised that as far and as fast as I could run, I could never outrun myself. Wherever I went, there I was. In the moments between the hustle and bustle I created, my intuition and inner knowing sat patiently waiting for me to repeat the same message: write and share your words and don't look back.

Writing has always been a sacred place for me. It's allowed me to alchemise the pain of my past experiences into understanding and compassion, and share perspective shifts that have cultivated ease, joy and love in my life. After running for as long as I could, I finally started to share my words online via Instagram, @ModernMind___. Quickly, I began to receive many messages about how my words had helped others to feel better about themselves and their lives, how the gentle guidance had opened up a world of possibility for change. I finally stopped denying my inner calling and allowed myself to be guided by my intention to help others.

This book is a manifestation of my life's purpose: to share my words, thoughts and reflections in the hope that they will lead you closer to yourself. Not who you feel you *should* be in order to receive love and validation, but who you *are*, beneath the expectations of the world. Closer to your core. Closer to your own innate calling and intuition. Because when we are close to ourselves and the vision we have for our lives, *we are naturally magnetic*. When we make our primary intention to feel good, we effortlessly attract positive thoughts, we reignite the fire in our bellies and invite transformative experiences into our lives. By attuning ourselves to notice different information, we begin to wire our brains in a new way. When it's natural to feel good, our point of attraction becomes aligned with more experiences, thoughts and emotions to affirm that reality.

You are a powerful creator. You may not currently be aware of that, or may have become so entangled in the fog and chaos of life and the thoughts of your mind that you have forgotten it. You may feel like your existence is dissatisfying or disappointing. You may have run so far from yourself that you no longer know how to find your way back. Perhaps you believe that this is just life. But what if there was more for you? What if your life could be filled with opportunities to feel joy and delight? *What if you discovered that you could attract more of what you*

When it's natural to feel good,
our point of attraction becomes
aligned with more experiences,
thoughts and emotions
to affirm that reality.

AMBER LYON — YOU ARE A MAGNET

*want – simply by focusing on it?*

But in the midst of social media, marketing and constant comparison, it's easy to only notice what's missing, feeling like our lives amount to no more than a second best to those we see around us. We've allowed our most precious resource – our attention – to land on what leaves us feeling disempowered and demotivated to create the life we dream of. But focusing on what's going wrong never gets us very far.

This book is for those who are willing to do the work. Those who are ready to attract possibility into their lens. Those who choose to walk the path that leads to changing thoughts and internal dialogue. To do the work that's necessary to deepen their relationships both with themselves and those they love. The work that's essential to feel good about life – not someday but right now – and envisage a future that's even brighter.

## You are a magnet – your journey starts here

We're all familiar with waking up on 'the wrong side of the bed'. The day that starts with us feeling a little off and tends to accumulate negative situations as the hours go by. Perhaps it's triggered by a restless night or a stressful week, but at times, there's no identifiable cause at all. Our sense of emotional balance becomes weighted in favour of frustration and agitation. It's as if this mood sends a signal out to the world letting every person and situation know that it's time to push our buttons. People push in front of us, things seem to take longer than usual, we step in dog sh*t on the way to work . . . the list goes on. Like a snowball rolling down the mountain, our moods seem to pick up situations to match them perfectly. One bad thing is followed by another, and another and another. And when we have enough of these situations back to back – on a loop, like groundhog day – we can find ourselves waking up the *wrong side of life*. The stress and anxiety of the days or weeks before are carried into each new day. We notice the same frustrations and same reasons to feel justified in our moods or behaviours. This process becomes so reflexive and so instinctual that feeling the way we do about our lives becomes a habit. To put it simply, we get stuck and there is no way of seeing the wood for the trees. There are no streaks of light on cloudy days to give us that sign that it's not a permanent state of being.

*But a new life is just one decision away.*

Our fundamental creative power in life is the ability to choose. To choose our thoughts, our habits, our behaviours, our relationships, our careers and even our identities. Although it may not feel like a choice to you right now, our habits and frames of mind can shape and solidify so much over time that they feel like concrete, immovable, inflexible truths of life that make us who we are, embodied in an all-too-familiar state-ment: '*That's just the way I am*'. This book provides the tools and resources to teach you that this is simply not true. Right here, in these pages, is your chance for change.

What would it look like to wake up on the right side of life? To have positive situations accumulate as you go about your day? For your touch points with the world to leave you feel-ing good and empowered? This simple shift starts within, by getting to know your own mind and the illusions it plays.

*The problems in your life are much less about the things that are happening, and much more to do with the way you see them.*

The power to change lies in learning how to harness the power of your magnetic mind. Then, you can face a fork in the

7

road where you've been before and make a new choice. It will take courage, patience and persistence but the journey will be rewarding beyond measure. You will have a life of your own, acting in alignment with your values, with deeper relationships and a stronger connection to yourself and your innate intuition.

## The magnetic mind

*We see the world not as it is, but as we are, or as we are conditioned to see it.*
Stephen R. Covey, American educator and writer

When I started to explore what this book would look like and title ideas, I kept coming back to the idea of a magnet, time and time again. Nothing else could represent the nature of the mind that I wanted to explore. Magnets are always attracting or repelling. We are no different. Like a magnet, when we change our point of attraction, we change what we pull into our lives. If we want to see change, we've got to start within.

Whether consciously or not, our minds have an agenda as we go about the day: to confirm the stories we tell ourselves about the world. These are a unique blend of familiar thoughts, past experiences and core belief systems we hold about ourselves or the world. They determine how we interpret things and the meaning we apply then becomes the reality we live in – our paradigms. Our paradigms determine which information from our environment we prioritise and where our focus naturally lands. As our magnetic mind screens our environment for evidence that validates the stories we tell ourselves and ignores the evidence that does not, our worlds suddenly become a reflection of *what we look for, rather than what is.*

So how do we see the bigger picture? How do we break free from our paradigms?

By slowing down, questioning our reflexive thoughts and introducing new stories and behaviours, we shift our inner narrative. We can introduce perspective shifts that turn our attention to the good in our lives, giving the mind a new directive: *to seek out the light.*

- Challenge becomes an opportunity to grow and evolve, rather than justification to abandon the path.

- Adversity becomes character-defining moments, rather than the route to feeling like a victim of circumstance.

- Pain becomes our purpose and passion to lead others out of the dark, rather than a reason to stay hidden from the light.

When I turned within and shifted my mindset, I watched my life blossom. What used to be a world full of suffering, disappointment and limitation became one filled with opportunity, connection and joy. And I want you to have the same experience.

*Each of the principles that follow invites you to reflect and change the way you think about your life.* To question the thoughts that you've always believed to be true. To create space between what is happening and how you feel. To lean into love, more than you lean into fear. You can magnetically attract the life you dream of – but you must first align yourself internally with that reality, training yourself to see it.

External changes always start with internal shifts. To change

External changes always start with internal shifts.
To change your life, you must start, quite simply, by changing the way you see it.

AMBER LYON — YOU ARE A MAGNET

your life, you must start, quite simply, by changing the way you see it.

## About this book: your four-part guide to magnetism

Magnetism is a relatively new term in the wellness world, but one I've always felt drawn to because it sounds like it feels – magic. It's a two-way relationship, acknowledging the role we play in co-creating our lives: not solely reliant on the external world to determine our inner state, but not so disconnected from it that we fail to take action and choose the new behaviours that are *key to meaningful change*. Whether consciously or not, we are co-creating our lives with our thoughts, feelings and responses to our external environment. Magnetism requires us to take responsibility for our internal world and how our inner state shapes what we experience.

This book will connect you to your own innate sense of magnetism, whereby you feel an ease and flow to your actions and positive outcomes from your decisions – a deep inner knowing that things are happening as they should, taking action from a place of joy and purpose, rather than trying to prove or force. Magnetism is all about acting in alignment with your authenticity and whatever vision you have for your life, letting go of the details around how it all unfolds.

Although it harnesses the power of manifestation (calling specific desires into your life), magnetism isn't solely about external attainment. The primary focus is to connect so deeply to your authenticity and what brings you joy that your outer world reflects and draws towards you more experiences that affirm this state of being. It's a small but powerful distinction.

It's grounded in the present moment, rather than in some future attainment or achievement. It's not to say you can't have the physical things you crave, but it's about simply knowing that those things are not responsible for changing your inner state – that your inner being is satiated by an ability to see the light in your life as it is now, and as it changes.

Magnetism is a state of mind – *a way of seeing the world* – whereas manifestation is a practice to call external things into our lives.

The magic of magnetism is that when we are truly connected to ourselves and our values, our whole world can shift overnight. There's no more trying to force things to happen, or sitting impatiently waiting for what we want to arrive, because we recognise that our lives are always a reflection of what we are now, rather than what we want. With this shift, life begins to glow in a new way and what we want effortlessly flows towards us because we recognise this moment is more important than our idea of what's coming next. The true power of change has only, and will only, ever be in this present moment right here.

I've seen this work help people in their darkest hours. Just recently, I received a message from a cancer survivor who let me know that the words and principles you are about to read here helped them to get through three months of chemotherapy. She said that the guidance gave her the strength and inspiration to move on from the experience. Having just celebrated her fortieth birthday with her three children, she told me that even in the thick of it, the simple perspective shifts had made the world of difference, her favourite being *one day at a time*. I share this story to let you know that even if you feel far from yourself, disconnected or lost in the midst of a great challenge right now, the words in this book will serve any and all stages of your life.

The primary focus is to
connect so deeply to your
authenticity and what brings
you joy that your outer world
reflects and draws towards you
more experiences that affirm
this state of being.

In the midst of my own inner struggles, these are the words and principles that I too return to daily in order to feed my soul and reconnect with my power.

## The guiding principles

Each of the essays in the book is centred around a 'guiding principle'. Consider these as fluid and adaptable signposts to what feels true to you. They are the framework and mindful reminders that I use to navigate life with more ease and grace, and I trust that they will serve you well, too. Return to the ones that resonate and leave the ones that do not. Keep them near by, as reminders to return home to yourself when you feel disconnected or consumed by the thoughts of your mind.

The book is divided into four parts that mirror the framework I use with my clients to tap into their most magnetic state:

- **Part One: Alchemising Fear** Here, among other powerful practices, you will learn how to distinguish between the fearful thoughts of your mind and your own internal guidance system, what your magnetic field is and how it impacts your world and how to see your fears from a new empowered perspective.

- **Part Two: Cultivating Courage** So much of our light is obscured by the doubts we have about ourselves and our beliefs about what is within reach. In Part Two, you will redefine what is possible by learning to trust your potential and capacity to fulfil it. You will learn how to tap into your intuition, to embrace every experience as a teacher and reclaim your power to change.

- **Part Three: The Magnetic Mindset** Part Three is all about the behaviours and perspective shifts you can use to embody your most magnetic self. We explore the rituals, routines and practices that help you to tap into your highest energetic state, while taking off the pressure to be anything other than yourself. In this section, we also explore what it means to have real self-worth, set an authentic vision and how to let go and trust what is unfolding, knowing that when you are clear on what you want, life brings it to you in mysterious ways.

- **Part Four: Living in Joy** When you trust yourself and trust in your life, it becomes natural to become more present, no longer living in the pain of your past or anticipation of the future. In Part Four, we explore the delight of being present with the simple pleasures of life – the joy that comes from being wholeheartedly yourself and owning who that is. This section will include finding joy in the simple pleasures of your life, how to spot the light in others and reconnecting with the awe of the world around you.

## How to use this book

Because each of you will be coming to this book from a different energetic space, there may be certain parts that resonate more or less, depending on what you are experiencing at any given moment. Therefore, you are welcome to read it from cover to cover, doing whichever exercises resonate with you, or, alternatively, immediately dive into whichever section speaks to you the most right now.

In this moment, a new life waits for you – one that aligns with your ultimate potential and constant delights. But in order to connect with this experience, you've got to be willing to see things in a new way. Each principle will guide you closer to this place and to your inner magnetism. When you change your energy, you change your entire experience. This, right here, is the beginning of that shift.

# PART ONE

# Guiding Principles for Alchemising Fear

# Don't Believe Everything You Think

Don't believe your thoughts.

Sounds counterintuitive, doesn't it? I remember the moment I first stumbled across this concept, many years ago in my early twenties. I was driving with the music at full volume, tears streaming down my face, curving along the twisted roads of a remote area of New Zealand. I was leaving a challenging relationship – one that had left me feeling second best all the time. Symbolically, the rain poured outside as hard as the pressure of the thoughts pelting my mind. In an attempt to pull myself together (plus, I had simply run out of tears to cry), I switched from the music to a podcast I had downloaded featuring Eckhart Tolle. He spoke softly and this quickly began to soothe me. For those unfamiliar with Eckhart, he is a spiritual teacher and author of *The Power of Now* – a powerful book on dissolving the ego and focusing on the present moment. Eckhart began to speak about the role of the mind and how it is separate from our core self.

Pause. *What?*

My outlook on life up to this point had been rigid. The way I saw myself and the world around me was as an exact reflection of the way I thought and built upon the accuracy of my assumptions. There was no thinking separate from myself because *I was my thoughts*. I used my logical mind to decipher the world around me, which had led to success in school and university. I had no reason to believe that my thoughts were anything other than an exact, accurate reflection of the world. This was the only secure thing I could hold on to in a turbulent world: the truth of my thoughts.

The trouble was, I was deeply depressed. So many of my thoughts about the world and why people behaved the way they did were justifications for why I felt lonely, insecure or incapable of achieving my goals. I never stopped to think that the problem wasn't the world, but rather, the way I saw it.

There is a sacred space between You (You with a capital Y being your core self and authenticity) and your thoughts. In this space, you filter the information from your environment and decide what it means. It's *crucial* to create distance between what is happening and your thoughts, feelings and assumptions about it. Because the less space you have, the more you assume your thoughts to be an accurate reflection of reality when more often than not, they are simply a justification for how you feel in the moment or reflective of an old story you may still hold. As you would with a sticker, you have to peel back your instinctual thoughts in order to see things more clearly. Then, the more space you create, the more you can begin to see that there is a separation between *what you think* and *what is happening*, between X and Y. When you acknowledge that your thoughts are observations, rather than accurate reflections, you leave just

When you acknowledge
that your thoughts are
observations, rather than accurate
reflections, you leave just enough
room to question them and
choose new ones.

AMBER LYON — YOU ARE A MAGNET

enough room to question them and choose new ones. Because your thoughts are *often not* as factual as you may have come to believe. The truth is, your inner dialogue is much more reflective of how you feel, and what you believe to be true, than it is an unbiased interpreter of a situation.

Imagine a mirror at a funfair – the type where you appear wobbly and distorted when you look at it. It's ridiculous and amusing because it is so clearly inaccurate. But this is no different to the *inaccuracy of how we see ourselves* and the world around us. If you saw yourself distorted in the mirror and believed it to be accurate, can you imagine how differently you would show up in the world? The type of negative self-dialogue that would follow? Would you hold your head high and walk confidently? Or try to hide away as much as possible?

Consider these thoughts for a moment: how have you seen *yourself* distorted in the mirror of life? In what way have you seen an inaccurate reflection of yourself? Pondering these questions not only allows your distorted reflections to emerge, but may be the first time you've acknowledged that how you see yourself and the world may not be the whole truth.

The mirror becomes distorted while we are children and don't know any better. It happens through comments made by parents or friends that leave us feeling ashamed or less than and they stick with us, making up our very fabric. We tend to soak up every little piece of information as a reflection of our worth and wellbeing. These distortions then become the source of all the limiting beliefs and stories we tell ourselves, about ourselves.

As adults, it's our responsibility to *transcend the limitations of our childhood selves*, leaving behind the distorted vision of how we've been taught to see ourselves and instead allowing ourselves to embrace a new vision – one that celebrates our authentic magic. It's no easy feat, but for each of us it's our own personal mission: to open the door to who we want to become, rather than continuously reinforcing who we've been; and by walking through this door, we give ourselves the opportunity to choose a new life, a new experience – one beyond the limitations of our past and what we believed to be possible, and one where it is natural to feel good about ourselves and our lives.

All this takes courage and patience, but I know you have both in spades – otherwise you would have never picked up this book.

 REFLECTION

The limitations we have come to believe about ourselves feel very real and true, but this is often because we have not stopped to question them.

1. What's one limitation that you've come to believe about yourself?

2. How do you know this to be true?

3. Can you find evidence that is contrary to this belief?

Guiding principle

# Becoming Aware of Your Magnetic Field

So much of our current experience is shaped by the habits of our past selves. If we want new outcomes, we must introduce a new way of being.

We each have our own emotional baseline – an emotional state that feels most familiar to us. This is a reflection of the feelings we tend to return to most often. Angry people tend to find a reason to be angry and happy people tend to find a reason to be happy. Consider this as your internal climate. Day to day, it may vary, but we tend to return to one emotional state more than others. Emotions trigger thoughts and the quality of those thoughts is what perpetuates our emotional state. Emotions alone, without the thoughts that follow, only chemically last around ninety seconds – isn't that unbelievable?

Just like anything else, the more we practise something, the more of an ingrained habit it becomes. When we regularly think and feel a certain way, we are rehearsing that mental and emotional state. But just because it's familiar, does not mean our baseline is always enjoyable. In fact, for many of us, feeling alone or not good enough is much more familiar than feeling confident and loved. Although it feels static, the way you feel about your life is simply shaped by the habit of how you've felt in the past. New feelings create new outcomes.

The thing is, your emotional baseline is not only an internal state, but it radiates from you and around you. What you feel inside is felt by others intuitively. I refer to this energetic space around you as your *magnetic field.*

*Your magnetic field = the unique energy that radiates around you, which is a reflection of what you are thinking and feeling in any given moment*

No two people have the exact same magnetic field, but they can be very similar. In fact, we tend to gravitate towards people, experiences and things that feel energetically similar to us. It often shapes the movies we like, the foods we enjoy and, in particular, the people we feel most comfortable around. When you are in a negative headspace, it's difficult and often triggering to be around happy-go-lucky people, and vice versa. Like attracts like. Whatever you are thinking and feeling shapes what is drawn towards you, and what you are drawn towards.

Your emotional baseline has such an enormous impact on your life because it influences not only your responses to situations, but also what your magnetic field is pulling in or pushing away. When you start to make internal changes and align yourself to a more loving, kind, considerate state of being, the world begins to respond to your energy in a new way.

To illustrate, try bringing to mind an experience you had recently with someone that you really love to be around. Take a moment to consider what you feel around this person. Conversely, bring to mind someone you know who is often in a terrible mood; you instinctively tend to create space from such people and when you are in close proximity to them, your whole body can begin to tense. It can feel like you are walking on eggshells, even if they haven't said a word.

With time, and with practice, you can shift your emotional baseline from one of fear to one of love. But it requires you to introduce new habits of thought – a new way of feeling, even if it seems strange or foreign at first. You may even hear the voice of resistance rise up and tell you 'this is pointless'. The mind resists change because it wants to remain in the realm of what's familiar. But when what's familiar no longer feels good, you must consciously push yourself to practise a new way of being in the world. And when you do so, you'll begin to emit a new energy from your core, attracting more loving experiences, people and situations into your life.

The key to change is always in awareness. The more aware you are of your current emotional state and the energy that you bring into any situation, the greater your capacity to redirect your attention more consciously.

## ✳ THREE WAYS TO RAISE YOUR EMOTIONAL BASELINE

1. Introduce a morning gratitude practice every morning by writing out three things you are grateful for in your life right now (they could be big or small things – just anything that brings you joy).

2. Share one compliment with yourself and one with someone your love daily (when we express kindness, we

Whatever you are
thinking and feeling shapes
what is drawn towards
you, and what you are
drawn towards.

radiate this energy and actively invite more kindness into
our lives).

3. When you notice your thoughts taking you down an old
   disempowering spiral, pause, place your hand on your
   heart and affirm: 'I no longer believe this story. I am a
   divine being and, in this moment, choose to return to love.'

Guiding principle

# Nobody Has It All Figured Out

In the past, I felt enormous pressure to have my whole life figured out: to secure work that lit me up, to find a passion, to have great relationships . . . I felt like everyone around me seemed to know what they were doing, while I was meandering through life, picking up and then putting down things that just didn't feel quite right.

I had this idea that there was one thing for everyone. Which meant that my purpose and passion in life were just hiding under a rock that I hadn't yet turned. The relentless search for this specific thing began to rule my life. If I couldn't find it, that meant my life didn't have true meaning. So the search continued, but over time, I grew gradually more faint-hearted, having found that nothing felt quite right, turn after turn. I was so focused on what I was looking for that I constantly felt that right now I wasn't where I wanted to be, but that sometime soon I'd arrive – once I had it all figured out.

Except no one has it all figured it – even when it appears so. In fact, if someone says that they do, it's often a good sign to run in the other direction. Each experience informs us of the

No one has it all
figured it – even when
it appears so.

AMBER LYON — YOU ARE A MAGNET

next step to take. Our passions are supposed to change and adapt as we grow and learn new things. It dawned on me that if I kept feeling I didn't have it figured out now, but that I would at some point, the more I moved forward, the further away that 'some point' would be. I saw the future me (a passionate, successful person) just a few steps ahead at all times.

I started trying on other people's lives and was left wondering why they didn't fit. But eventually, as I became clearer on what didn't work, I also started stumbling across what did – little clues of joy and curiosity leading the way.

Each time I trusted my curiosity and picked up a skill that didn't necessarily show a clear path forward, I started to create my own life. Slowly, the skills I was acquiring began to mesh together in unique ways and make more sense. In time, I had the exact tools necessary to fulfil unique work opportunities that seemed almost magically tailored for me. Now, as I look back, I can appreciate that I couldn't have mapped it all out from the beginning. Each skill was built on the one before and informed by different chapters of my life and unfolding curiosity.

It's overwhelmingly tempting to walk a path when we know the destination (even if it's an unsatisfying one) – to seek constant clarity and validation at every turn. The unfamiliar and unknown are the roads less travelled. Our sense of direction is only guided by how we feel, which is something that we've been taught comes second to the certainty of the rational mind. But not all paths are immediately clear, and although it's scary to walk a path we're not sure leads anywhere, that's what life asks of us. To trust that we're going to be ok walking in the dark.

It's natural to feel the pressure to figure things out, even though you don't have all the answers. But the more comfortable you become with *not* having the answers, the less pressure you will feel and the more you will be able to naturally flow with where your life wants to take you.

## ✻ FOUR REMINDERS WHILE FINDING YOUR OWN PATH

1. Trust your curiosity and where it leads you. (You don't have to make sense of everything right away; it will make sense in time.)

2. Let things unfold naturally. (You'll know what to do when the time is right; there's no rush to figure it out right away.)

3. If you feel you can't figure something out, it's likely because you do not have enough information right now. Spending all your energy thinking without sufficient information leads to mental stress and anxiety. (Take a moment to practise deep breathing: inhale through your nose for a count of 4; exhale through your open mouth for a count of 8.)

4. Affirm: 'I have all the answers I seek for the present moment. I allow each experience to inform me of the next best step to take.'

Guiding principle

# At Any Moment, You Can Choose to Show Up in a New Way

Some of my earliest memories revolve around stories told to me by my mother when I got into bed each night. I'd get lost in the tales she would tell, finding myself mesmerised by certain characters. This quickly evolved into watching movies and replicating the characters I saw on screen. I'd try on different roles to see how they felt. I was constantly trying to find myself in the world around me – who did I want to be? A doctor? A mechanic? An artist? A musician? In childhood, there are no bounds to the creativity of identity. Wanting to be a vet one day and a painter the next is perfectly reasonable; in fact, why not both? Being open-minded in this way is endearing.

But as we grow and evolve, our need for love and connection becomes our foremost priority. As a result, we tend to shift our focus from who we *want* to become to who we *have* to become in order to receive the love and attention we crave. We notice the roles, actions and behaviours that receive the most attention and reward. And although these behaviours are primarily based on the satisfaction of others, they can end up becoming the things we value the most in ourselves. Then, rather than exploring traits that may feel more natural or embody a more accurate reflection of our true selves, we end up restricting our identities to what we've decided is the best route to connection. Suddenly, who we've had to be to connect and fit in becomes who we identify as.

*True self = a true and authentic expression of who we are and how we feel in any given moment*

*Survival self = the roles, behaviours and traits we've had to assume to receive love and acceptance*

This is a perfectly natural response to growing in any environment. Just as a new seedling will bend and grow towards sunlight, so we grow towards the source of the most love in life. But what do we do when the person we had to be to receive love as a child cannot function in the adult world? When who we've had to be no longer fits with who we want to be?

Have you ever tried drawing a circle around an ant on a piece of paper? The ant, which was wandering around freely just moments prior, now seems to be trapped within the little circle on the paper. This is a powerful visual analogy for our self-identity; it's just a little circle we've drawn around ourselves. We are not really trapped by it, but it can feel that way at times, if we don't remind ourselves that there's a whole world around it.

Perhaps you were the kind and quiet kid in class, celebrated for being a high achiever. Maybe you were applauded for being a great athlete and the centre of attention at social events or you were commended for being an emotionally resilient and independent child. This accepted version of yourself becomes the natural default. It's tried and true, and it feels safe to operate within it because you've already determined it to be a reliable route to receiving love and acceptance from others. So it makes perfect sense that when you feel called to explore a new expression of yourself, it feels unnatural. It's terrifying to embody something that you cannot be sure will be celebrated by others. But the space you are caught in, between who you feel safe to be and who you feel called to become, is the invitation to expand your identity.

The truth is, no role, trait or relationship is large enough to fit the entirety of who you are. When you define yourself to be more of one thing and less of another, you restrict your human experience. You are a boundless being by nature. The only restrictions are those you have imposed on yourself. But what if there was a new space for you to expand into?

For a long time, I identified as an intensely independent person – it was a core pillar of my identity. When I was growing up, my parents simply did not have the capacity to carry my emotional needs, so I strapped them to my own back and got on with it. As an adult, this manifested as me being fiercely defensive to offers of help in any area, despite an inner craving to let people in so I could share the load. I'd decline the help, acting in tune with my strong, independent character, while suffering through the intense burden of feeling alone during difficult times. I rejected any notion that I needed anyone but myself. As you can probably imagine, this wasn't a winning strategy. In fact, I damaged relationships by preventing my friends and family from showing up for me when I needed them most. But I was caught in the space between who I'd always been and who I wanted to be – someone with the capacity to let others in. I desperately wanted to share my fears, stress and vulnerabilities with those I was closest to, but my sense of self kept me confined to my independent identity.

After many years of going through life alone, I realised something needed to change. The person I had defined myself as no longer fitted with who I wanted to show up as in the world. So little by little, inch by inch, I pushed the boundaries of myself outwards. I would ask friends to show up for me in little ways – like picking me up on the way somewhere or letting them know when I was stressed. In becoming a fuller expression of myself, I needed to surrender who I had always been.

*Surrender statement = 'This is no longer working for me; I open myself up to finding a new way of showing up in the world'*

Although it can feel terrifying to introduce a new part of yourself to your life, the world will not implode. Rather, what happens is that the world will always make space for you to show up in a new way. You will always have as much space as you choose to take. If you feel restricted, you are simply not giving yourself enough space to occupy. If something no longer works because you are showing up in a new, more authentic way, this is a signal that it no longer serves you and your path forward. Think of this as a deep spring clean: to create space, some things will have to go. But always remember, those are the things that were keeping you small.

As you expand into a more authentic expression of who you

No role, trait or
relationship is large
enough to fit the entirety
of who you are.

are, you will notice how spacious your mind, body and soul feel once they can express themselves more honestly. In fact, if you are growing, you will continuously evolve and expand. As your identity becomes open and spacious like a child's once again, you will be reminded of the liberation of choice – that at any point you can choose to show up in a new way.

## ✳ FOUR REMINDERS FOR WHEN YOU FEEL AFRAID TO EMBODY A NEW VERSION OF YOURSELF

1. Who you had to be to receive love and acceptance as a child is no longer who you have to be to receive those things as an adult.

2. No one else will give you permission to be your true self but you.

3. When you own who you are fully and wholeheartedly, you inspire those around you to be more truly themselves.

4. Whatever you lose through showing up more authentically is making space for more aligned connections and opportunities to enter your life.

Guiding principle

# Free Yourself from Your Past Decisions

Looking back over your life with the knowledge you have now, as an adult, it's easy to pass judgment on how you handled certain situations or to berate yourself for what you could have done better. 'If only I had known . . .' That's the beauty of hindsight – it's easy to see your mistakes clearly when they've already unfolded.

When you judge yourself in this way, you are effectively shaming your past self for not knowing what you know now. And because you can't go back and change things, you carry that shame with you into your present experience. Instead, once you've apologised for what you did wrong (if needed), you have to release yourself from the pain of your past decisions. You did the best you could with the knowledge, resources and information you had at the time, and just because you may have more knowledge now, that does not mean your past self deserves continuous punishment.

Reflecting on your past so that you can make better informed

Every decision triggers the exact events necessary for your personal growth journey.

future decisions is how you ensure that you don't repeat old mistakes. But it's critical that this reflective practice remains a judgment-free experience. Whereas knowledge empowers you to adapt for the future, shame disempowers you, trapping you in your past.

What has happened has happened. Punishing yourself or continuously reminding yourself of what went wrong, or thinking over the countless ways things could have been different '*if only*', wastes all the energy you could be spending on thinking on what could be *now*.

Forgive yourself for what you did when you did not know any better. You are now equipped with all the knowledge you need to make better decisions in the present moment. Every decision triggers the exact events necessary for your personal growth journey. Each and every one serves a higher purpose. You are learning, and that is all that is asked of you.

 ## AFFIRMATION

'I forgive myself for my past mistakes. I no longer choose to carry any judgment for what was. I am now making decisions aligned with my highest good.'

Guiding principle

# Are You Choosing Love or Fear in This Moment?

Our thoughts only have one of two origins: love or fear. Our most loving thoughts are signalled by a sense of connection, belonging and compassion, while our fearful thoughts are signalled by a feeling of separation, judgment and justification. The goal is not to try and control the endless river of thoughts that enter your mind, but, instead, to fine tune your awareness to recognise the difference between the currents and where each takes you.

Our fearful thoughts tend to lead us into the rapids of our minds: we judge others, we find reasons why we are right and why someone else is wrong, we justify our actions and limitations . . . Each fearful thought leads to the next, and when we believe and act on them, we create a ripple effect of that fear throughout our lives. Fearful actions trigger fearful responses. This often leads to arguments with the people we love, unkindness to ourselves or others and a general unsettling feeling.

Our loving thoughts exist below the rapids. They require

us to step back from a situation to see things more clearly. Where our fear wants to divide, the loving part of us wants to connect. Where fear tends to judge, the loving part of us extends compassion. Where fear shuts us down, the loving part chooses to remain open. Loving thoughts search for evidence of how similar we are, what we could do better and how we can positively contribute. When we act on them, they bring us closer to those we love and ourselves, encouraging a peaceful mind.

But loving thoughts are not nearly as reflexive. We have to train ourselves to choose new thoughts. If the narrator of your mind has been largely steeped in fear, loving thoughts will feel alien at first. But as with anything, awareness, patience and practice will pave the way for a new habit.

When you become aware of what your personal fearful thoughts sound like, this will help you to recognise them when they inevitably pop up. And when you do so, you can consciously practise redirecting your river back to love. Because at every moment you are either moving closer towards or further away from the most loving part of you – the sacred space beneath your fears that is connected to all of life.

Without judgment, you can reflect on the list below to see if you recognise some examples of your own fearful mind in action:

- Finding all the reasons why you are right and why someone else is wrong

- A need to prove your point

- Judgmental thoughts about yourself or others

- Making assumptions about someone's behaviour and what it must mean

- Taking things personally

- Shutting down others' opinions

- Feeling jealous of what someone else has

- Feeling insecure or not good enough as you are

- Feeling you have to do something special or achieve in order to be valued

- Trying to convince people to like you

These are just a few signals that the fearful mind is at play. Throughout this book, I'll be guiding you through the journey of shifting out of fear and living in a state of love. For now, when you recognise or notice these thoughts in your own mind, you can use the following affirmation to be grounded back in love and redirect your energy into connection and peace.

## ✳ AFFIRMATION

'I no longer choose to channel my energy into thoughts of fear. In this moment, I now choose to redirect my attention back into love.'

The goal is not to try and control the endless river of thoughts that enter your mind, but, instead, to fine tune your awareness to recognise the difference between the currents and where each takes you.

AMBER LYON — YOU ARE A MAGNET

# THREE WAYS TO DISTINGUISH BETWEEN FEARFUL AND LOVING THOUGHTS

1. If I act from this place, does it connect me or disconnect me?

2. If I speak from these thoughts, are my words warriors of love or of pain?

3. If I believe these thoughts, am I empowered or disempowered?

Guiding principle

# More Is Lost by Indecision than the Wrong Decision

How many times have you become so tangled in your thoughts about what to do that you end up taking no action at all? I've seen it in myself, and in countless friends and family close to me. Perhaps you have an inspired idea or something that feels exciting and novel – say, a career change, a business idea or a curiosity for a new hobby. The idea carries a sort of energising quality, as though giving you the momentum to take the first step towards it. But then the inevitable happens: your logical mind begins to tear it apart, so that what was once inspired now seems downright deluded and impossibly inconvenient.

As someone who identifies as a rational thinker, one of the most valuable lessons I've had to learn is when to *not listen* to my logical mind's conclusions. If having big ideas that are quickly shut down by your own reasoning is something that resonates with you, these words are for you: *thinking alone will never take you where action will.*

When a new idea pops into our minds and we think through

The only way
to know for sure
is to get out
in the thick of it.

it *too much*, we begin to place all of our past reference points on to what may or may not happen in the pursuit of it. Although we cannot possibly begin to imagine what might unfold, it is our mind's job to anticipate what *could*. And when we listen to its thoughts, we often snuff out an idea before it has a chance to breathe its own air.

It is more important to take action than to get it perfect. Often what kills our desire to get started is the idea that we have to get it right. But the truth is, we lose more to indecision than imperfect progress. On the way to any goal, you learn what you need as you go. In order to see if an idea has any merit, you've got to be willing to give it a go before you know exactly how it's all going to work out.

My reasoning mind has always been my safety net. I've spent countless hours ruminating on which decision to make or what next step to take, not realising that my overthinking was simply a mechanism to not act at all. It was much easier for me to sit on my bed and think through what might go right or wrong than to actually be out there in real life, figuring it out via the experience itself. But the only way to know for sure is to get out in the thick of it.

Although you might feel you need to think things through to their logical end before you take your first step, this exact line of thinking will kill your ideas before they have a chance to stand on their own. Instead, what if you gave them a chance before you snuffed them out? Without the momentum of action, you deprive yourself of the motion that allows the wind to catch your sails. So while you may not have the full plan or understand where the next step will lead you, trust that the action you take will always lead to where you need to be.

# 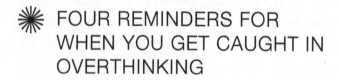 FOUR REMINDERS FOR WHEN YOU GET CAUGHT IN OVERTHINKING

1. Taking action will always give you more clarity than trying to figure it out in the isolation of your mind.

2. You don't need to know how to do step six or seven when you are on step one.

3. If you want new experiences, you have to be open to taking new actions.

4. Trust that the magic of your life exists in not fully understanding what will happen next.

Guiding principle

# Your Dreams Require You to Show Up before You Feel Ready

This book began many years ago – a collection of essays I pulled together from five years of writing. It was a secret project; one that I didn't dare speak of to others, mostly out of fear that the voice of doubt would validate my own deep fear that my dream was an unattainable fantasy. Despite having a rough draft, I waited. I waited for the moment when I felt prepared to finish it. When that moment didn't arrive, I figured that if it was meant to be, something would happen that would trigger my return to that draft. That moment never came either.

We've been taught to wait for external cues for internal pursuits. But the truth is, we have to pursue whatever we feel called towards before we have the invitation.

In 2018, my life was going in a completely different direction. I had started a career in property development with a small firm in my home city, and although I enjoyed the work and the

51

team, I knew deep down that it was the safe choice. We are all familiar with the safe choice, whether it's a career, a partner or a way of living; it's whatever keeps us in our comfort zone – the realm of the known. But when we restrict ourselves to the safe choice, we reinforce the walls between what we know and what we do not, and the higher these walls become, the less likely we are to try new things, connect with new people or pivot in our careers. Waiting for an invitation to pursue what you have in your heart is asking life to break through these walls while you hide behind them.

The dreams we have in our hearts ask us to venture into the unknown – into the world of possibility. You will have your own dreams that lay latent in your being. Ones that you may have come to deem unattainable or unrealistic. But consider this for a moment: these very dreams would not be in your heart if you did not have the capacity to fulfil them. You may have been waiting for the world to ask you to begin, but you only need say yes to yourself. To question it less, and act on it more.

When I eventually did come back to that rough first draft, it was years later. It wasn't that I felt ready; it was that I realised that the feeling of preparedness only comes after you begin. You do not have to feel ready or prepared to take the first step. Simply: if you wait till you feel ready, you might miss the opportunity altogether.

Readiness is an illusion. You have to give yourself permission to pursue what's in your heart even when you feel underqualified for the task. You must walk forward while you still carry your fears, doubts and disbelief in your heart – because it is through your actions that you gain the exact skills you need in order to feel prepared for the next step.

If you wait till you feel ready, you might miss the opportunity altogether.

# 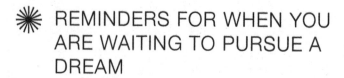 REMINDERS FOR WHEN YOU ARE WAITING TO PURSUE A DREAM

1. You may never feel ready to pursue what's in your heart.

2. No one else will give you permission to live your life in a way that pleases you; you must give yourself permission, even when it feels scary.

3. The realm of the known is a collection of your past experiences. If you want a new experience, you must explore beyond your comfort zone.

4. The experience of discomfort is not a sign to turn back; rather, it is a sign you are entering the realm of possibilities.

5. Your dream is sacred. Pursue it for yourself and protect it from the opinions of others.

6. Let yourself indulge in dreaming.

Guiding principle

# Make The Most Of What You Have

Your whole life happens in the moments between what you have now and the next major milestone. If you fixate solely on the milestone, the majority of your life becomes a means to an end. Time will keep slipping through your fingers, as the anticipation of what's to come takes priority over what's right in front of you. In waiting for some future circumstance, you take your most precious resource (your attention) and place it where you are not; this can leave you unbalanced or anxious, relying on outcomes you can't control.

What we can control, however, is how we show up to this day. The attitude we bring to this day determines what we are attuned to notice most. We don't experience our lives; we experience what we focus on – and when we focus on what's missing, we inevitably feel disempowered and demotivated. The fastest way to feel terrible about our lives is to focus on all the ways in which it's not how we'd like it to be. This leads us to low-level thoughts of comparison, jealousy and judgment. That's not to say that we shouldn't crave for things to be different – just that *the power of change is not fuelled by focusing on the obstacles.*

Making the most of what we have is all about looking at our lives and seeing all that already exists, rather than all that does not. Our energy is best spent focused on the skills, relationships and capacity we already have so that we can create change from an empowered place.

You can shift your focus from what's missing to what you already have by seeking out the joy and resources that are already present and available to you. If you are craving deeper connections, could you reach out to those already in your community to spend more quality time together? If you are looking to build a business, how far can you go with the skills you have now? Is there someone you could reach out to for advice over a coffee? Instead of finding all the reasons why you can't, what if you redirected your focus to what you can do?

This simple shift attunes your energy to notice opportunities and connections that can help you to see new solutions to old problems. Suddenly, you are not building from scratch, but building upon the foundations you already have.

Your life will start to glow in such a way that you will no longer feel the need to fixate on the light on the horizon. Because all the good you crave is here right now in its deconstructed form, if only you take the time to put it all together. Let the warmth radiate through.

 ## AFFIRMATION

'I am surrounded by an abundance of support and resources. I have everything I need to get started.'

Guiding principle

# Answers Always Live In the Present Moment

The desire to know what happens next rules us all. If only we could peek behind the curtain and see what our lives will be like in a month, a week or a year. If we could have a little insight into how things would turn out, we'd know exactly where to place our attention, what decisions to make and which steps to *take now*. Helping us answer the all too familiar questions: is this the right job for me? Is this the right partner? Am I doing what I'm supposed to be doing with my life?

But we can't leap ahead and figure things out before they've even begun. Although it sometimes seems like it would be much easier if we could, this would rob us of the delight, surprise and spontaneity of all that's in store for us. Answers reveal themselves little by little as we continue on our paths. There's no way to figure out exactly where we will end up because each moment sparks the *possibility of a new destination*. Stopping before those answers and trying to prematurely figure it all out doesn't serve us because we have not yet had the experiences to inform us.

So how do we create a life that feels rewarding, fulfilling and joyful? By following the things in our lives that already align with these states of being.

The need to jump ahead and figure out what may or may not happen will take you out of the present moment. And when you are out of the present, you are also out of touch with your energetic radar to what feels good. It is only in the present with each experience that you are guided to move a little closer to some things and further away from others, magnetically moving towards or away from what is most aligned with you. If you preset the destination, you'll be unable to adapt in the way you can when you let each experience inform you of the next step to take.

There is no one path for you. What makes your path right is that you are on it. The key is to become less focused on ideas about how things *should go* and more attuned to how things *are going right now*. Grounded in the present with your current experiences, you'll have the exact information you need to take the next best step. Trust that when you are present and aligned with what feels joyful, you may just end up somewhere even greater than you could have imagined.

There is no one path for you.
What makes your path right
is that you are on it.

## ✳ PRESENT-MOMENT DECISION MAKING

1. How can I let this moment inform me of the next best step to take?

2. What feels most aligned with my values?

3. If I let go of my expectations on what may happen, would I still choose this?

Guiding principle

# We Tend to Resist
# What We Need Most

Although external challenge is very real, the space where we face the most troublesome resistance is not outside of us, but within the confines of our own mind. It's the inner dialogue we hear when we start to consider taking the next step in the direction of what we truly desire. Procrastination, the prioritisation of everything else, the inability to sit down to do the work . . . All this is the resistance that we must overcome – the inner resistance to what we know is the next best step.

It's not the act we are resisting, but the parts of ourselves we must face to move forward. Taking action requires us to question the illusion that we cannot, or that we are not capable. Action requires us to trust in ourselves more than we ever have before and have faith that life will support us. This is why we resist what we know is best – because it requires us to let go of the limitations that we have come to believe about ourselves. Taking action in the face of resistance requires us to act in alignment with new beliefs *before we believe them*.

When we manage to take action not in the absence of but in

When we manage to take action not in the absence of but in defiance of our inner resistance, we have broken free from our past limitations.

AMBER LYON — YOU ARE A MAGNET

defiance of our inner resistance, we have broken free from our past limitations.

Anything that really means something to us will likely terrify us to our cores, but we can either delay and avoid, or move forward, knowing that no fear exists without an invitation to expand.

## ✳ FOUR REMINDERS WHEN YOU ARE RESISTING POSITIVE ACTION

1. It will always feel strange to show up in a new way; your resistance and avoidance of taking new action are a natural reaction to staying in the realm of the familiar.

2. Your inner resistance only has power if you listen and believe its thoughts. Just because your mind tells you that you cannot, or should not, does not mean that this is true.

3. You can act separately to what the mind tells you and, by doing so, you reinforce a new belief system.

4. What feels difficult now will, in time, become your new normal. But in order to reach that point, you have to push past the initial resistance you feel.

Guiding principle

# You Get to Choose How You Respond to Challenge

We each have the power to choose how fear manifests in our lives. We can soothe ourselves through it or it can consume us. Either way, the end result is the same: *we must move forward.*

When I was twenty-two, I moved to Istanbul on the advice of my agent to help build my modelling portfolio. A perk of going to a secondary market to model (somewhere other than fashion hubs like Milan, New York or London) is that you are more likely to book highly competitive editorial work – the type that can make or break your career. I agreed to a place-ment in the city for two months and saw the experience as a new adventure. Who would turn down the chance to explore a foreign place in the guise of 'working'?

In fact, it turned out to be much less work and much more waiting around in the agency's van, moving from casting to casting. We'd be expected to be downstairs early in the morn-ing, out front of our little three-bedroom apartment, shared by eight girls, and often wouldn't be back till the late evening.

We'd drive across the city from location to location, spilling in and out of the van, casting books in hand. There was little to do to keep entertained other than stare outside the van's windows and observe the city, its people and surroundings.

The streets of Istanbul are steep, narrow and usually one-way. Often, there are large vans parked either side of the already very tight streets, leaving only centimetres either side of the travelling cars. I found myself on one of these little, narrow streets one particular morning, waiting in the van as other girls were still inside the casting. An older man stood in the middle of the road, just past the narrowest point, to help guide the approaching cars. I sat and watched each driver who passed through.

Some laughed with the man, inclined to trust him, but perhaps somewhat dubious of his traffic-control skills. Some sped through effortlessly, paying the man no mind at all. Others yelled and screamed that someone should come and move the other vans, certain that they couldn't pass through, while a few started and stopped on the brakes so forcefully that their cars jolted, causing them to bump the cars either side.

As I watched, I was able to observe how the exact same challenge provoked different responses in each person.

We all face situations that require us to trust life in some capacity. In these times, although we may feel powerless, what we still have control over is how we move through our challenges and the parts of ourselves that we call forward. In other words – which part of ourselves do we allow to drive the car?

Challenges, disappointments, setbacks, delays, roadblocks, change, rejection are all inevitable experiences in our lives. Instead of hoping they don't happen, our energy is better spent preparing and understanding how we can best respond when they do. And if we don't check in and set our own standards, we will use our default reactions – ones that may not be conducive to our growth, progress or peace of mind.

It's not denying the fact that we are afraid as we navigate a challenge, but it is simply deciding that this part of us, the fearful part, will not be driving the car. They may very well be in the car with us, but we can choose a more grounded energy as our driver. It will take conscious effort, but simple practices like slowing down and connecting with our breath can create enough space to choose how to respond in a new way.

You can practise this now by bringing to mind a situation that usually frustrates or irritates you. Close your eyes and imagine yourself in that situation. Now imagine yourself choosing a different driver: how could you handle this situation and remain in your power? What part of you would best navigate this specific challenge? Imagine yourself navigating this frustration from this new energetic place. Now you have a roadmap for how to navigate this challenge in a new way, and you can put it to the test when you next encounter the situation and see what happens.

Loving reminder: we can't
control life or its circumstances,
but we can control how we
show up to the challenges
we will inevitably face.

# A SIMPLE PRACTICE FOR WHEN YOU FEEL FEARFUL OF A CHALLENGE

1. Give yourself a moment.

2. Bring your attention to your breath, slowing it down, so that you can think more clearly.

3. When you feel grounded, make a choice: how will I show up to this challenge? (Which part of yourself would handle it with the most ease and grace?)

4. Close your eyes and imagine the most capable version of yourself navigating the situation or challenge. Notice how you carry yourself and how you approach the situation. Put this into practice and see what outcome follows when you bring the best of yourself forward. (Mentally imagining a situation before it occurs helps to prime our minds to respond in a new way.)

Guiding principle

# Every Relationship Ebbs and Flows

You know that feeling in your gut when you sense that little disconnect between yourself and someone you love? When, for no apparent reason, things seem different – they don't have that same organic flow that they once did. Something now feels static, disjointed or forced. Most of all – it's *disorientating*. How did you go from being two peas in a pod to all of a sudden being awkward around each other? As much as you try, you can't direct the relationship river back into the dynamic flow you once so peacefully drifted along in. The space between where you are and where they are becomes a circus for the mind, making it difficult for you not to spiral into yourself. But when space comes up, it is your invitation to turn within – to take your energy away from the emotional distance between you and another and into the closeness with yourself.

All relationships ebb and flow. It's natural for there to be moments when we feel far away from those we love. What a precious reminder of how much we appreciate them being so close. Feeling distant doesn't always have to mean something, unless we make it mean something. Sometimes all we need is a little space to see our relationship more clearly. It could be a process of falling apart in order to fall back together, like so many things in life.

Sometimes people are so caught up in the happenings of their lives that they reflexively pull back for their own emotional processing of something that may have nothing to do with us at all. But regardless of the cause, when someone pulls back, it's a reflection of the fact that they need space – and boy oh boy, can this be a triggering experience.

Space can be frightening because it looks on the surface like we may lose someone we love, and sometimes it makes us aware that we've lost ourselves in the relationship. We can get so inter-twined that we lose the distinction between who we are and who we are in a relationship. Emotional distance gives us an opportunity to check in and see if we still have a strong sense of self, separate from our relationship to another. Do our lives still feel full? Or do they revolve around this one person?

When we connect well with someone, it's easy to place an unrealistic pressure on that one relationship as the source of our happiness and connection. When that becomes threatened by physical or emotional distance, it's deeply unsettling because not only could we lose our person, but also our source of joy.

When someone pulls back, it gives us an opportunity to see how far we've pulled forward. The more panic that rises when someone we love pulls back, the more we have likely emotionally travelled for that connection. The extent to which we are fearful of this space is the distance we have to travel back to ourselves.

Here are a few reasons we feel afraid when someone we love pulls back:

- We have placed disproportionate pressure on this one relationship to meet our needs

- We have negotiated on what we authentically want in order to keep the connection

- It triggers an old limiting relationship belief from childhood (such as the fear of being abandoned by someone we love).

It's important to remember during these periods that what is yours will never slip between your fingers. What is meant to remain will always remain. When we wholeheartedly trust that life is always working in our favour, we can trust that the right people will always show up in our lives.

When space does inevitably pop up, it's also important to be mindfully aware of whether we are showing up for the people we love in the same ways we expect them to. Are we supporting their goals, the dreams they have for their lives? Are we celebrating their wins, and holding their hands through the troughs? Because just as we want the best relationships for our own lives, we must also hold ourselves to this high standard.

The way to close a gap is always through communication. Instead of letting your internal story run rampant in your mind, slow down and check in with yourself. Reflect on why this space feels unsettling to you. Can you sit with it for a moment? Can you speak to it? Once you have clarity on your internal state, can you seek clarity on their perspective? What do you need in order to bring your energy back into yourself?

Let your internal guidance system give you the answers by building in moments of stillness to your day, like meditation, freehand journaling or a long walk. Once you have clarity with

When we wholeheartedly trust that life is always working in our favour, we can trust that the right people will always show up in our lives.

AMBER LYON — YOU ARE A MAGNET

your own internal state, your energy will be grounded rather than reactive, which is conducive for connection and communication. Let the person in question know that you've observed more space and gently ask if there is a reason why. Start an open-ended conversation and let yourself travel to where that needs to take you both. Although communicating during such an unsettling time can feel frightening, it will always bring light to the situation, and it is this light that will lift the anxiety that you hold in the pit of your stomach.

##  MAGNETIC RELATIONSHIP SHIFT

1. Write down the worst-case scenario from what is bringing you anxiety in this relationship. Then, check in with yourself: despite the emotional pain, would you survive?

2. What is one thing you could you do this week (separate from this relationship) to bring more joy, light and love into your life?

3. If there is space in your relationship, what is it that you are hoping this other person will do? Is there a need of yours that you are quietly expecting them to meet? Can this need be met in another way? How could you give to yourself what you are seeking from them? Write down one thing you can do this week to move closer to this outcome.

Guiding principle

# Breaking Free from Anxious Thoughts

One of the keys to breaking out of an anxious thought loop is awareness. We cannot change what we are not conscious of. The practice of becoming more aware simply involves checking in and observing how we are feeling more often. The simple act of noticing allows us to redirect our attention if we no longer wish to be in an emotional experience; it's not about avoiding our emotions, but understanding ourselves well enough to know when we are naturally processing them – and when we are unnecessarily feeding into the fearful mind.

## ✳ SIX STEPS TO BREAK FREE FROM AN ANXIOUS STATE

I have a very simple guide that I use with my coaching clients to interrupt the inner dialogue of anxious thoughts, soothe the fear and release the resistance that's causing mental turmoil:

The simple act of noticing allows us to redirect our attention if we no longer wish to be in an emotional experience; it's not about avoiding our emotions, but understanding ourselves well enough to know when we are naturally processing them – and when we are unnecessarily feeding into the fearful mind.

1. Stop what you are doing and bring your attention to your physical body.

2. If you are not already, sit up and roll your shoulders up and down.

3. Now, bring your attention to your breath: close your eyes and begin taking deep inhales through the nose, sending the air down to the pit of your stomach, and long exhales through the mouth. (When we shift the focus from mind to body, we interrupt our mental dialogue.)

4. When you start to feel physically relaxed, take a moment to ask your body: 'What do you want to tell me right now?'

5. Trust whatever intuitively comes through. If nothing comes through, or you feel like it is taking too long, just bring your attention back to your deep inhales and exhales. Trust that the answer will come through when it's ready.

6. When you feel like you've taken enough time to listen to your body, reflect on what you need in this moment to feel supported. Could you provide that for yourself or reach out to someone who could help?

Guiding principle

# Relationships Are Mirrors to Our Inner Worlds

A strange thing happens when we are upset with someone, whether that's our boss, our partner, a friend or even a stranger: we often place the blame for how we are feeling on them. We tend to outsource responsibility for our own emotional state to someone else because sometimes it can feel too painful to hold it all by ourselves. *'It's your fault I'm feeling this way'. 'You make me feel like . . .' 'You are the reason I feel . . .'*

But what if this wasn't the whole truth? While at times, another's actions may not be favourable towards us, we *always* get to decide how to respond. Yet the more hurt and insecure we become as a result of someone's actions, the more difficult it is to turn within, often leading us to react out of our triggered state.

Relationships are mirrors. They have the ability to reflect back at us where we may still be carrying hurt, shame or pain from our pasts. They can trigger us into a state of such reactivity that we are left confused about where our actions and words have even come from.

One of my favourite spiritual teachers, Michael Singer, speaks about this beautifully in his book *The Untethered Soul*. He suggests that each of us has little thorns stuck under our skin from past experiences. When someone bumps or touches one of our thorns, we recoil in pain, stating, 'Don't touch my thorn!' But what if we could instead remove the thorn, releasing the need to make our internal pain someone else's fault?

We need to first acknowledge the responsibility we have for our reactions. We've got to release the habit of blaming the world for how we feel, and instead decide to take control of our lives.

*You are responsible for you*

*You are responsible for your actions and words, regardless of the trigger*

*You get to choose to respond, rather than react to situations, people and the circumstances you find yourself in*

When you take total responsibility, you also liberate yourself. You give yourself total freedom – freedom to choose how you feel, independent of circumstance. But what about the thorns? What about the parts of yourself that are painful to touch – those insecurities that you hold from childhood and past experiences? Every time life touches those painful parts, you are being called to shed the limitations of your past – more fully to accept and love all parts of who you are, not just the parts that feel easy to love.

Like magnets, we are always attracting towards ourselves people, situations and experiences that reflect back to us the next lesson in our personal-development journeys. Each person and experience we come across acts like a mirror, allowing us to more deeply understand ourselves and what we may need to heal.

Next time you are triggered, turn within and ask yourself: what fear in me is this other person or situation triggering? Maybe it is the fear that you are unlovable, or that you will be replaced. Perhaps it is the fear that you will be abandoned or that you are not wanted. Insecurities stem from our deepest fears. The fears that we all share in varying degrees with one another – that, in some way or another, we are fundamentally flawed, and it's just a matter of time until others figure it out. But this is not true. The only flaw we have is that we cannot see ourselves clearly as the wondrous, light, infinitely worthy beings that we are.

*Past: I feel pain because of this external situation*

*Reframe: what is it within **me** that is making this external situation so painful?*

To release the thorn from under our skin, we simply choose not to react to the pain when it is being touched. After a while, the pain will slowly begin to subside. Just like a prickle under the skin, the less we touch it, the less irritated it becomes, until naturally, in time, it works itself out from under the skin.

Nevertheless, as you navigate this new way of responding to the world, you may still experience internal pain triggered by your environment. When you feel the pain begin to rise, ask

What matters is not how many times you slip up, but how many times you are able to correct yourself and your thoughts.

AMBER LYON — YOU ARE A MAGNET

yourself: what do I need to give myself in order to no longer feel this way?

For me, a lot of the time it's simply a case of being heard, or giving myself an extra moment of love and kindness. You'll be amazed to see the insights and healing that take place when you learn to meet your own needs in any given moment.

It may feel unnatural or difficult to begin taking responsibility for how you feel – to realise you hold the power. You will have moments when it does, in fact, appear like it absolutely is someone else's fault that you feel the way you do. But still, you ultimately get to decide how you react. To take back control. So you can either spend your energy on frustration, resistance and disappointment or put that same energy towards understanding, healing and growth. It doesn't mean you don't respond – just that you give yourself the opportunity to make a choice on how you wish to navigate forward, instead of leaping ahead based on habitual reactions.

What matters is not how many times you slip up, but how many times you are able to correct yourself and your thoughts. With repetition of new behaviour and ways of thinking, you are consciously rewiring your brain to behave in a new way. With time, it will become your reflexive response to turn within, rather than attack outside when you are triggered.

## ✳ FOUR REMINDERS FOR WHEN YOU ARE TRIGGERED

1. You don't need to respond straight away. Take as long as you need to decompress and come back to your emotional baseline before you respond.

2. Before blaming another for how you feel, ask yourself: what is this situation or person triggering within me?

3. When you take total responsibility for your inner world, you also claim total freedom to choose how you feel separate to your circumstances.

4. Every person and situation you find yourself in is your teacher. What is this situation trying to teach you?

Guiding principle

# Be Honest.
# Be Kind. Be Direct.

Being honest is arguably one the scariest things we can do, especially when it comes to the people we love. The idea of rocking the boat can be so overwhelming that it can lead us to inaction. We put our heads in the sand and pretend that if we don't acknowledge it, the problem might just go away. And it does. For now. But the words we feel but do not share tend to accumulate, and the more we go on avoiding how we really feel or what we really want to say, the more layers begin to cement between us and the person we care about.

I can't tell you how many times I've allowed a relationship to deteriorate because I wasn't brave enough to be the first to acknowledge something wasn't right. How many times have you been with someone you care about and your feelings have been hurt by something they've said or done, but you've said nothing? In those moments, you've abandoned yourself *and* the connection. Running from difficult conversations and uncomfortable truths blocks you from having deep, meaningful connections with others.

Sharing the truth of how you feel is not about outsourcing

responsibility for your emotions. A lot of the internal work you have to do is to try and decipher whether you are feeling upset about something real or if it's your own insecurities playing tricks on you. But no matter the cause, without the clarity that comes from communication, you leave yourself to the assumptions of your mind's one-sided narrative.

Healthy relationships require the capacity to have difficult conversations. To sit with one another and understand that although you may not always agree, you look beyond right and wrong to try and understand one another. True love says, I see you, I hear you and I accept you as you are. When we allow ourselves to speak openly and honestly with those we love, it creates a sense of safety in the relationship. Knowing where you stand with someone is incredibly healing, especially for those of us who may not have had clear communication in our relationships growing up.

Although it may frighten you to speak your truth, the outcome of a difficult conversation is more often than not a closer connection. Once you get over the initial resistance to speaking up, you'll set a new precedent for your relationship – one of honest and clear communication.

Without the clarity that
comes from communication,
you leave yourself to the
assumptions of your mind's
one-sided narrative.

AMBER LYON — YOU ARE A MAGNET

# ✳ FOUR TIPS FOR OPEN AND HONEST COMMUNICATION

1. Remember that deep connections are built on the capacity to have difficult conversations.

2. Remain open to seeing things from another perspective.

3. Focus less on being right and more on how you can connect and understand one another.

4. Unspoken words accumulate, so speak up in the moment, rather than leaving it for later

Guiding principle

# Are You Prioritising What Really Matters?

It's so easy to get caught up in what we are doing with work or our social schedules and end up neglecting our most cherished relationships – the ones with people who are by our sides through thick and thin, the people we can count on to be there for us no matter what. Why is it that these are the people we so often take for granted?

As rewarding and important as it is to remain open to new connections and foster new relationships, there is something to be said for tending to our *'lifers'* – the ones who have seen every stage of our growth and stayed with us along the way. It might be a parent, a childhood friend, a sibling, partner or a chosen family – they are the ones that we can turn to in our lightest or darkest hour.

When you tend to your micro world (the life you live privately), your wellbeing truly blooms. By investing in your closest relationships, you equally invest into your own wellbeing – because your relationships are the most significant contributor to your general happiness.

The delight in life lives within the everyday moments – the morning coffee you share with your loved one, the laughter late at night with friends. External accomplishments and busy social calendars never truly compensate for missing the all-too-precious ordinary moments with those you love. When all is said and done, these are the people who remain by your side – and what could be more important than that?

## ※ REFLECTION

1. Take some time today to reach out to one of your people. Check in on them. See how they are doing, and whether there's anything you can do to bolster them. Sometimes just a supportive message is enough to begin a ripple of love in your social pond.

2. As you consider how you can best show up for others, also reflect on whether you are showing up for yourself. Are you supporting yourself, so that you have the capacity to give to those around you? If not, could you schedule some time in this week to do something that fills your cup?

External accomplishments and busy social calendars never truly compensate for missing the all-too-precious ordinary moments with those you love.

Guiding principle

# Tapping into Your Internal Guidance

You have an abundant resource that you may not be aware of. It's an intelligence available to you at any moment that helps to solve problems, come up with creative solutions and give clarity on tricky situations. It's your own personal internal GPS: *your intuition.*

Our intuition is based on what we know to be true by feeling, rather than our intellectual reasoning. It taps into the intelligence of our body, rather than just the knowledge of the mind. As excellent as our minds are to solve logical problems, we so often use them to solve the problems of the heart, reasoning through decisions that would be better informed by our intuitive intelligence.

Trusting intuition is not acting without thinking but *acting on feelings.* Some people refer to it as our instincts – what we know to be true before our minds have the time to process how or why.

See if you can recognise your own experience of intuition in the examples below:

- A feeling of 'knowing' something to be right for you, before you have the evidence to prove it

- Feeling a pull to go into a certain shop or cafe and finding something there you've been looking for

- Changing direction or taking a different route home when an area feels unsafe

- A strong hunch that someone is being dishonest or unfaithful

- Knowing that something is off between you and someone else before it is spoken

- A clear idea to pursue something new, seemingly out of nowhere

- A physical sensation of 'yes' to an opportunity, person or experience

But it's tough to trust. We are not taught about our intuition in school – about how and when to use it. In fact, our intuitive hunches – those little inklings about pursuing certain ideas, starting new projects or changing course – are often not the most logical choices at all. They may not make sense to others, or even to our own rational minds. They may require us to make difficult decisions, which would be otherwise all too easy to avoid.

As with many things, you have to build trust through repetition. You may not feel ready to trust your intuitive guidance on larger pivots or major life decisions just yet, but you can start by tapping into it with little questions like: what is my body craving nutritionally right now? Or: which way should I drive to work today? Then, instead of allowing your rational mind to come up with what makes the most sense, see if you can wait

As excellent as our minds are to solve logical problems, we so often use them to solve the problems of the heart, reasoning through decisions that would be better informed by our intuitive intelligence.

a moment and hear what your body has to say. Perhaps you'll land on the same answers, but perhaps not.

When I introduce the concept of intuitive guidance with my clients, many will ask: 'But what about when I feel anxious before a test, a flight or insecure with my friends or partner? Is that my intuition, too?' It's important to be able to discern between fearful thoughts and intuitive insights. If you are confused, you can refer to the list below for clarity:

**Fearful thoughts:**
- Focused on past or present experiences
- Assuming the worst-case outcome
- Triggered by a situation
- Come from the constant stream of thoughts aka our 'thinking mind'*
- Triggers a feeling of anxiety in the mind and body

**Intuition:**
- Only ever in the present moment
- Feels like a new idea or solution
- Seemingly comes out of nowhere
- A sense of calm in the mind and body

**\*Thinking mind** (what Zen Buddhists refer to as the 'monkey mind', which is the constant stream of dialogue we have about ourselves and the world around us).

The more time you take to listen to your intuitive insights, the more frequent and clear they will be as you become more familiar with them and what they sound and feel like to you. Build trust in their intelligence by acting on them and seeing what follows. Treat it as a playful experiment with life, and see what you learn along the way.

## ✳ THREE WAYS TO TAP INTO YOUR INTUITION

1. While getting dressed in the morning, instead of picking out a familiar outfit, ask yourself: what would bring me the most joy to wear today?

2. Sitting quietly in meditation without any music or guidance, ask yourself: is there anything I need to know in this moment? Don't judge what comes through, or if nothing comes up at all – this is simply about creating a container for insights to come through.

3. Take more time to reflect before you respond. When you slow down, you create more space between each thought and that's where your intuitive guidance can come through.

## Guiding principle

# Are You Investing in Yourself?

When I get snappy or find myself stuck in judgmental thoughts about myself or others, its often a signal that I've been neglecting the practices that make me feel my best. Life gets busy and, as the pressure to 'get things done' mounts on a certain task or project, I'll often end up neglecting my precious self-care rituals (perhaps meditation or a morning walk outside) in order to spend time ticking things off my to-do list. But our self-care practices are our foundation and should be what we lean on when things get busy. They don't take away from our ability to be productive – if anything, they make it possible for us to show up for what needs to be done from a more energised place. I've come to think of my daily rituals as depositing into my energetic bank account – in other words, investing in myself.

Your energetic bank account is topped up by the practices or habits that leave you feeling restored, replenished or energised. No amount of 'savings' would be too much. The more you have in your account, the more ease you will feel in staying grounded, and the faster you will be able to redirect your energy to a state of love when triggered. Then, when stressful times inevitably arise, you have something available to draw on. When you have no habits or practices that replenish your energy, it's natural to feel more anxious, unsettled and overwhelmed during busy times. This is what I refer to as an *energetic overdraft*. An energetic overdraft is the experience of resisting any and all action (including behaviours we know are good for us) because we have are too drained, mentally, physically or spiritually. If you find yourself in an overdraft, focus on rest. Once your physical body has had some time to recharge, you can bring your attention back to your positive habits.

By making time each and every day for practices that connect you to yourself and make you feel good, you add to your energetic resources. When you begin, you may not notice a huge shift, but the everyday effort accumulates.

Examples of simple practices that can add to your energetic bank account are as follows:

- The Morning Waterfall (write one full page every morning when you rise in order to clear the clutter of the mind).

- Meditation (set a timer for 5–10 minutes, closing the eyes, breathing deeply and scanning your body).

- Taking a walk in nature.

- Listening to an inspiring podcast (some of my favourites are *Super Soul Sunday* by Oprah and *On Purpose with Jay Shetty*).

- Listening to and speaking affirmations (a few of my favourites: 'I am divinely supported in life,' 'I am loved,' 'I am and always have been worthy of my dreams.').

Your energetic bank account is topped up by the practices or habits that leave you feeling restored, replenished or energised.

- Going on a solo date once a month.

When we start to implement a new habit, it's really hard to let go of the expectation of immediate results. It may take days, weeks or even months to consciously notice or spot a difference in energy levels and mood. Like watching grass grow, it can feel like things are moving painfully slowly. But remaining consistent with any habit is reliant on your ability to defer gratification. What may feel challenging or difficult now is paving the way to feeling good in the long term. Just as saving requires a sense of self-discipline and consistency, so do our self-care practices. And although you may not feel immediate results, trust that one day, not long from now, you will wake up and it will seem natural to feel magnetic, energised and excited for the day ahead. That is your signal that you've been doing the work. So focus less on a desire for immediate results and more on the ways in which you can continue to top up your account today.

## ☀ THREE REMINDERS FOR WHEN YOU ARE STARTING A NEW SELF-CARE PRACTICE

1. The way to close the gap between the life you have now and the life you crave for yourself is through consistent action.

2. The work you put in today will be enjoyed by your future self.

3. Every little bit of effort accumulates.

Guiding principle

# You Are the Captain of Your Soul

As a child from a single-parent home, with a father addicted to drugs and entangled in a life of crime, I felt powerless growing up. I was strapped into a constant emotional rollercoaster, moving homes eighteen times over my first eighteen years of life. The lives of those around me felt like storybook fantasies compared to the stress and anxiety that became my normal. It wasn't until I turned eighteen and moved into my first little flat (shared by two others twice my age) that I began to get in touch with what my life could be, separate from what I had always experienced.

With my new-found independence, I dived into self work for the first time, turning inward to discover the truth of myself and what I dreamed of. I learned to meditate, I began journaling daily, took the time to explore new hobbies, interests and books that opened my mind to new ways of being in the world and found new role models to follow.

One particular afternoon I was listening to an interview with

At any moment you are capable of changing your story because you are the one writing the next chapter.

AMBER LYON — YOU ARE A MAGNET

Oprah Winfrey in which she quoted the poem 'Invictus' by William Ernest Henley:

*I am the master of my fate,*
*I am the captain of my soul.*

On hearing these words, something awoke within me: a sense of power that I could change, *and that I would change*, so that I could live a life of joy. The change required to create what you dream of is only a willingness to see things differently to how you have in the past. It's not what's happened to you, but what you've made of it that determines how you feel and the outcome of your life. In taking responsibility for your life in its totality right now, you also take responsibility to create what you want, instead of allowing your reflexive responses and past habits to pave your future.

The life I've built today is no reflection of what I saw growing up or what I used to believe was possible. I wake up next to a loving partner, with a connection that is stable, honest and filled with respect. I live in a peaceful home, with no raised voices and only kind, direct, truthful words. I have a successful career doing what I love most. But, most importantly, there is a peace within myself – deep inner knowing that everything is going to be ok. I am capable of finding the light no matter the darkness . . . because I am the light.

*That is magnetism.* The ability to attune your attention to the information that leaves you feeling empowered, confident and aligned. The knowledge that your response yesterday does not have to be your response today. That at any moment you are capable of changing your story because you are the one writing the next chapter. What you are looking for doesn't come from without, but from within.

Life dances with this magnetic energy.

My heart yearns for my younger self. Tears come to my eyes at the very thought of letting her know just how good it's going to get and how ok she's going to be. And for you, too, anything and everything is possible. As you enter the next part of this book, bring this spark of possibility with you. You are going to need it for the courage required to meet the parts of yourself that may be holding you back from all the light.

## ✳ WRITING A NEW STORY

1. Sit down with a pen and a blank piece of paper.

2. Think of your life from a third-person perspective and write out a movie bio about it. Include any patterns you seem to experience in your life – things that have happened repetitively, both good and bad. Think about your intimate relationships with friends or your partner; write about the sort of role you play – are you needless? Needy? Controlling? Distant? Try not to judge what you write and be as honest as you can.

3. Next, write out another story – one you would like to live, with the types of relationships you'd like to have. Don't place any limitations on it.

4. The first story is one you have inherited; the second is the journey your inner being is asking you to take.

# PART TWO

# Guiding Principles for Cultivating Courage

## Guiding principle

# Feeling Lost Is a Calling Home

I think at some point or another all of us can relate to the feeling of being in limbo – not knowing where we are going and not feeling quite happy with where things are right now. It's as if we are floating in space, disconnected from the world around us, when nothing quite lands, nothing means as much as it used to and we've lost touch with the magic of life – a strange mist separating us from joy, delight and those we love.

Despite the internal dialogue that's perhaps telling you otherwise, these times are natural. They are necessary for growth and key to discovering a fuller expression of ourselves. Experiences of confusion and disconnection are crucial in realigning us with where we are supposed to be.

Anyone who embodies the fullness of themselves without apology has at one point or another drifted from the truth of who they are and had to find it again. Being lost is the gift of learning how to find our way back to ourselves and our magnetic cores. Because sometimes it takes losing ourselves to rediscover who we truly are.

When I first moved to New York for modelling, I was

wide-eyed and majorly idealistic. Somewhere deep down, I had a small inkling that it wasn't what I wanted to spend my life doing, but I had grown up idealising the iconic faces spread across magazines. So I continued to pursue this, despite my intuitive hunch that it wasn't for me because I thought *eventually it would make me happy*.

I sacrificed important parts of myself in an attempt to emulate what I thought success looked like – a cool, aloof persona that barely resembled my goofy, giggly self. The more I mindlessly chased each job, the more hollow and empty I began to feel. I became totally detached from who I was and what actually brought me joy. I was so busy trying to be someone that didn't feel authentic to me that I didn't realise how far away from myself I had travelled. I vividly remember not understanding how I'd got to this place and having no idea how to get out or where to turn.

If you are feeling lost, one of the first steps is to acknowledge and accept where you are. Although it may feel heavy and unpleasant, it is an essential step before moving in a new direction. In a world that so loudly tells us the right and wrong turns to make, it can be easy to mistake others' directions for your own. After a while of listening to conflicting information (what you should be doing, what others are doing and what you want to do), you can end up pretty far away from your own authentic truth.

A lot of the time, we follow a path because it meets a need we have in the moment. But that need may come from a very scared part of ourselves, prompted by a limiting self-belief. Our limiting beliefs are false truths, things we've come to believe about ourselves or our lives that outsource our power. They are built on the belief that our value is determined by the world around us, and when we act on them, it's easy to drift down inauthentic paths.

The needs of our limiting beliefs are never fully satisfied. There's never enough money, validation or external love to fully satiate our deepest fear that we are not enough. And so down we go, further and further along a path that fundamentally doesn't make us happy or reflect what we feel placed here to do.

When we are lost, we are invited to look at the destination we set out for and why. In my case, modelling was a Mecca of validation. I grew up believing that if I became successful or well known, my father would *finally* regret not being a part of my life. It fed my belief that I needed to be something other than just myself to be loved.

You can explore your own intentions with the following reflective prompts:

- What are you working towards right now in life?

- Why? What is it you are hoping to feel in attainment of this goal?

If you knew you were infinitely loved and supported, no matter what, would you still choose this path for yourself?

When we follow a path based on limiting beliefs, our intuitive self will often try to signal that something's amiss. If you are living out of alignment, your internal guidance system has likely been issuing mayday alerts. Just as your internal guidance system can give you clues on what to pursue, it also lets you know when you are pursuing things that fundamentally are out of alignment with your inner being – little signals that the path ahead is not in tune with your highest good and purpose. If you ignore your intuitive insights – that feeling of disconnection, unease and general dissatisfaction – you shut down your ability to redirect your course. Although it can be difficult to face the reality that you may have pursued something that no longer feels good, it's much easier than the pain of continuing to live an inauthentic life. So once you know you're off course, how do you find your way back to yourself? In order to find solutions, we've got to shift out of the thoughts and limiting beliefs that are opposing them. This means resisting the urge to loop on thoughts like: 'I feel so lost,' 'I don't know what to do,' or 'I don't have any answers.' Focusing attention on the problem only solidifies it because when you are too attuned to it, you end up blinding yourself to all the solutions and opportunities radiating around you. I always think of this as 'problem tunnel vision'. When we focus on what's going wrong, we tend to only find evidence that reinforces the problem.

Instead, try affirming to yourself: 'I accept how I am feeling,' 'I release my resistance to what is,' and, 'I am now open to creative solutions'. These statements open up the mind to seeing information that may not have been visible previously. If you tend to be more cerebral and find yourself stuck in your thoughts, call a trusted friend to chat. They may bring light to something you could not see by yourself. Each of these actions channels your energy towards movement and solutions, rather than entangling you further in negative thought processes.

Next, when looking for a new direction, reflect on the following questions:

• What have you always been naturally really good at?

• What do friends/family seek you out for help or advice on?

- What could you spend all day on and not think about the passing time?

Or, if the answers to these questions feel out of reach, try, simply:

- What's one thing you could do today that you enjoy?

These probes help to remind you of the things that bring you closer to yourself. The simplicity of building one thing into each day that feels good will do wonders. *I promise.* And as you master adding one thing to your daily routine, try adding another, and another and another. It could be as simple as leaving a little earlier for work, so that you can sit down to peacefully enjoy your coffee, enjoying the serene bliss of having a quiet moment to yourself before taking on the day, rather than drinking it on the go. Perhaps you can start a new hobby that you've been putting off because there always seems to be something else more pressing. In prioritising little moments that allow you to connect to your personal expression of joy, you move closer to your magnetic core once again. And when you are close to yourself, you are always at home, no matter where life takes you.

## ✳ FOUR REMINDERS FOR WHEN YOU ARE FEELING LOST

1. Disconnection from the world is a manifestation of feeling disconnected from yourself and what you enjoy; these are perfectly natural emotions and present you with an opportunity to realign with yourself.

2. Check in and ask yourself: *Am I focusing on the problem, or the next best step?*

3. Building in things each week that bring you joy is the fastest way to return back to yourself.

4. Be kind to yourself during this time.

Guiding principle

# It's Only Natural to Doubt Your Potential

It's easy to look at those who are high achievers or doing well in their field and assume they must have total confidence in themselves. How else could they show up so seemingly effortlessly? It's an assumption we all make – that somehow these people must not be plagued by the same internal struggles that we are, and that we must be different, more flawed, than most. I held on to this belief for so long; it was my justification for why I could not show up for what I dreamed of.

Doubt is a slippery thought; it's difficult to pin it down and really hold it in our two hands. It sneaks into the mind and lurks beneath the surface. It's that snarky tone that creeps in and shuts down every attempt at progress. It loves to point out why we are inadequate or underskilled for the task at hand. Why we are, in fact, merely imposters. Doubt manifests in the thoughts that we all know only too well – the type that keep us frozen in inaction, unable to walk towards our calling.

But instead of seeing doubt as evidence that you should not

Doubt is fear. And the remedy for fear is listening to what it has to say and soothing it with kind, reaffirming words.

AMBER LYON — YOU ARE A MAGNET

continue, what if you saw it as uncomfortable company along for the ride? If it's going to be present no matter what, why not make it a friend? Instead of resisting each questioning of your ability or worth, try to allow the voice of doubt to come into your mind and let it be heard. Instead of arguing, what if you extended loving compassion to this fearful side of yourself?

Ultimately, self-doubt comes from a place of love. It's just the part of ourselves that is afraid of how things will turn out. It's the part that's afraid of our own light. But when we acknowledge that doubt will accompany every stage of our evolution, it becomes easier to make peace with its presence. In fact, self-doubt is a sure sign that we are expanding into new spaces. The presence of doubt signals that we are embarking on new territory, a new adventure into discomfort. We can reframe doubt from a fresh perspective – one that is rooted in loving compassion for all parts of ourselves. Doubt is fear. And the remedy for fear is listening to what it has to say and soothing it with kind, reaffirming words.

## ✳ EMPOWERING YOURSELF

1. Remind yourself of experiences you've had in the past where you've felt the same way – times when you doubted your ability or capacity to make it through to the other side.

2. Next, remind yourself of each experience where, despite the doubts that flooded your mind, you made it through. Maybe you even thrived on the other side of that experience.

3. You may often see what you are facing as uncharted waters. But you've likely been here before and you'll be here again. Doubt is not going anywhere, but your belief in what it's saying can be lifted.

## ☀ LOVING PRACTICE FOR SELF-DOUBT

Next time you feel doubt rise when trying something new or embarking on a different path, practise extending compassion to yourself. See if you can soothe the doubtful voice with words of love and reassurance. Affirm: 'I'm going to be ok; I will take it one step at a time.'

Guiding principle

# You Are Either Evolving or Resisting

There are few more excruciating experiences than when something that has become a part of who we are changes. It's the type of pain that goes so deep to our core that it feels as though we might shatter like a cold glass exposed to hot water. Except the parts of you that feel like they've scattered across the floor were never really you to begin with. They were just familiar.

Change forces our hand to surrender the parts of our lives that are no longer needed in our personal development journey.

We've all been there . . . a relationship we were deeply invested in taking a turn for the worse, seemingly out of nowhere; being let go from a job we adored; having to move out of a home that has been our safe and secure nest. All this fills us with fear. A part of ourselves seemingly lost in the process of letting go of something we've come to assume would remain the same for ever. When things that we've come to accept as a part of our identity and worth change, it can feel like we are being stripped of who we are. It's very natural to identify with what you do, where you live and the relationship roles you have, but when that becomes all of who you are, the integrity of your identity becomes based on the ever-changing world around you. When these things then inevitably change and evolve, of course you feel torn, disconnected and disappointed, focusing on what you've lost, rather than what that space could now be abundantly filled by.

We are hardwired to crave predictable circumstances and align ourselves with what is familiar, emotionally and physically. It gives us a sense of security and certainty when life gets out of control. The trouble is our craving for consistency and predictability is in opposition to the impermanence of everything in life. It's a scary thought, especially when we have good things in our lives, that they may not remain that way for ever. It's ok to wish that they would – but that frame of mind can become the bedrock for pain when we *expect* things to remain the same. Even the best things in life, the type that last a lifetime, evolve and shift as we grow and develop. If we expect things to remain the same, whether good or bad, we exist in resistance to the *great unknown*.

'The great unknown' is how I refer to the experiences that exist just past the curtain of this present moment. We know what's been, and what is right now, but it's impossible to predict what will come next. In fact, when we try (often projecting what's already been on to our future), we limit our capacity to see new opportunities and rob ourselves of appreciating the impermanence of things as they are right now.

The great unknown can be interpreted in one of two ways: absolutely terrifying or exciting. It all depends on how you choose to see it, and if you are open to the idea that things could be better than they are now. When we tightly hold on to the idea that now is as good as it's going to get, any change becomes unwelcome.

It's not about needlessly replacing the details of our lives or taking them for granted while idealising what could be, but remaining open minded to the ways our life is unfolding before us. Instead of holding on to what was, opening our hand to what could be. A tightly closed fist cannot receive and perhaps the very change you fear is making space for something greater than you could have imagined.

Here are a few examples of how change can help us to grow:

- It can open our minds to seeing a relationship in a new light, allowing room for it to evolve and for someone to show up in a new way. It's an opportunity to grow together, instead of growing apart.

- It can allow us to release relationships that have come to be toxic and unfulfilling, making space for more aligned connections.

- It can be the catalyst to a career pivot or seeking out a new, more fulfilling role.

- It can be an opportunity to redefine who we are and what we value about ourselves.

You may not feel very hopeful right now, especially if you are in the thick mess of losing something that feels so a part of you. But the key to navigating change lies in your ability to recognise that there is something beneath all of the roles you play in life. This place, and your ability to connect to it, will give you an infinite resource of strength, perseverance and trust. To know that who you are, at your core, is unchangeable by any external circumstances. The certainty that no matter what happens, and what changes you may navigate, you have *yourself* to return to.

It may appear to be the breaking of your world as you know it, but the beauty of destruction is in the rebuild. The parts of you that are on the floor may have felt like you, but they were never really the truth of your being. There is nothing that can be robbed of your eternal essence. You get to pick and choose the pieces you will use to create your new world. You can either try and replicate and repair the one that has been or build something new.

So what do you want to create this time? Which parts of yourself will you leave behind? Which will you build on once again? Let yourself embrace the pain of change and the grief you may have for the life that once was. Let it strip you of what you have come to assume you were, exposing the core of yourself that is unchangeable – capable of navigating any situation and circumstance. No role, relationship or circumstance is large enough to fit the entirety of who you really are. Your world is meant to change. Beautiful as it may be now, it is not destined to remain the same. Change brings along with it new ideas, new energy and new opportunities. Change is the ripe, fertile ground for the seeds of your mind. Change is a handwritten invitation to the great unknown. Will you accept? Or will you resist?

What courage it takes to love and release what has been and simultaneously make space to love what's next.

# Change is a handwritten invitation to the great unknown.

AMBER LYON — YOU ARE A MAGNET

# ☀ VISUALISATION

1. Hold your hands out in front of you, palms facing upwards.

2. Closing your eyes, imagine holding your life in your open palms (your circumstances, relationships, things you are working towards, your expectations and desired future outcomes).

3. There will be certain things in your life that you tend to control more than others. Imagine those things in your hands: the things you most want to control or are most afraid of changing. Squeeze your fists tightly over these things.

4. Next, imagine trusting that your life is always working in your favour, bringing you the most aligned relationships, opportunities and circumstances.

5. As you feel this trust growing, internally say to yourself: 'I release the need to control my life. I am divinely supported and guided.'

6. Release the grip of your hands.

7. Open your eyes and notice if you can feel a sense of relief in your body or mind.

Guiding principle

# We Are Both Light and Dark

I used to be terrified of the dark. As a child I'd sleep with a giant teddy bear over my face, as if I could block out the darkness of the night. I remember my mother sitting with me one night as I went through my usual routine of asking for the lights to be left on. She told me, 'The darkness becomes much scarier when you are unwilling to look at it.' Then she turned off the light and we looked around the room together. After a while, my eyes adjusted to the change and I could see my room more clearly.

Seeing our own shadow (the parts of our personality we've rejected) is a bit like allowing ourselves to sit in the dark. It's about looking at what frightens us, so that we can tell the shadow from the illusion. Our shadow is what we are most afraid to be true about ourselves. It's the limiting, negative beliefs that live in the darkness of our minds. For me, seeing my own shadow involved sitting with what I thought to be the ugliest parts of myself (my need to control, my physical insecurities, a feeling of 'brokenness'). The parts I was ashamed of that made me want to crawl into a ball and hide at the idea of anyone finding out about them.

But the more hesitant we are to look at the aspects of ourselves we've come to reject, the more power they have over us and our ability to sleep peacefully. Here are a few questions to help you reflect on what your own shadow may be:

- What traits do I most reject in others?

- What would be the worst thing for the world to know about me – something I work to keep hidden or well managed?

- What am I most afraid people think about me?

The truth is that as scary as it may seem at first, the more we look at something, the less frightening it becomes. The fear comes from the unknown nature of the hidden self. But the beauty of looking at these things is that we begin to notice, in the light, that they aren't monsters, after all. In the light, they are just different parts of ourselves that have been rejected and isolated. And once we can see these parts or beliefs about ourselves more clearly, we can start to look after them.

I cannot express how crucial this is for our health and well-being. If we have parts of ourselves we reject or don't accept, we give so much of our power away. The shadow self is not something to be rid of. It begs for our acceptance and compassion. The parts of you that you may have learned do not belong in the world, which you may have hidden, are still an authentic part of who you are. True confidence and spiritual health come from accepting that we aren't perfect. There are parts of who we are that may not be inherently easy to love, but that does not make us any less worthy of the love we seek.

If we can sit with the parts of ourselves that we've been so

There is nothing more magnetic than someone who has made peace with all parts of themselves.

AMBER LYON — YOU ARE A MAGNET

afraid to show the world, we allow them to reintegrate into the wholeness of who we are. We are no longer divided by the seen and unseen. We have the capacity to show up in any environment, with all our facets intact, unafraid of what might be noticed by the world. There is nothing more magnetic than someone who has made peace with all parts of themselves. Each part of who they are (the good and what we perceive to be bad) makes up an authentic whole human being. Each part is a wonderful complement to the next.

The aspects of yourself that have been hidden may have been there for a very long time. They might be afraid to come out and see the light of day. They may not trust that it is safe. Take it slowly, this is not something to be rushed.

## ✳ FIVE REMINDERS WHEN LOOKING AT YOUR SHADOW

1. Take your time; you do not have to look at everything at once.

2. If it feels too confronting to look by yourself, seek out the support of friends or professional guidance.

3. When you face what frightens you most, it becomes much less frightening.

4. Integrating your limiting beliefs and what you've come to reject about yourself is key to showing up more authentically and magnetically in your life.

5. Place your hand on your heart and affirm: 'I lovingly accept all parts of myself. Every part of who I am – even the parts I have come to believe are difficult to love – are worthy of love.'

Guiding principle

# Heavy Feelings Can Be Intuitive Messengers

Whether triggered by circumstance or our emotional reservoir, we've all been hit by a wave of difficult-to-manage emotions. This can look like crying in the car, trying to steady a shaky voice when asked 'Are you ok?' Feeling alone, despite being surrounded by other people. Something is off. Everything is as it was, yet something has shifted inside. Somewhere inside we ache for something we can't quite define.

The thing with emotions is that they do not come out of nowhere – even if it may feel that way at times. In fact, when heavy feelings appear, they come from below: below the business of our lives and distractions we may have sought out. Our magnetic self is always speaking to us. Sending intuitive whispers that we are living in alignment, or nudges that we are not.

When the world around us no longer feels like enough for us to feel good, we are called to turn within and understand why. And as tempting as it can be to look for answers outside of yourself, turning inwards will always deliver your highest

When the world around us no longer feels like enough for us to feel good, we are called to turn within and understand why.

guidance, uniquely tailored to what you are experiencing.

When we are suddenly down in the dumps, there are a few general causes – reasons for brewing emotion beneath the surface to which we can't attribute a source or a purpose:

- Accumulative inauthentic action (living a life of *shoulds*)

- Latent past emotions (past experiences we have not processed)

- Lack of joy (things feel heavier when we don't put them down)

## Accumulative inauthentic action

When you take one step away from what you feel intuitively pulled towards in favour of what seems to make more logical sense, you move one step away from your authentic path. And while just one step by itself won't take you very far from your truth, if each of your decisions throughout the day (35,000 on average) takes you one step further, you can end up so far away it becomes difficult to find your way back.

I always like to think of acting in alignment with myself as my magnetic core. When I'm close to my core, it's easy to make decisions that feel good and align with my higher path, despite my fears or resistance. But the more I act on what I feel like I *should do*, in favour of what I truly want, the less I am in tune with my energetic radar of what feels right. Think of a time in the past when you've been really consistent with going to the gym or moving your body. Did you notice how much easier it was to find the motivation to go over time? And perhaps other positive health decisions – like choosing to eat a healthy alternative or going to bed earlier – felt easier, too? Now consider a period of not exercising at all. How much harder was it during that time to eat well and look after yourself?

The same can be said for the choices we make about our careers and relationships. Do you feel inherently aligned with what you do for work? Or is it just a way to pay the bills? Do you feel connected to your spouse or friends in a deep and meaningful way? Or are they relationships that simply make sense and are convenient?

Inauthenticity can affect every aspect of our lives. In fact, inauthenticity in one area, usually signals that it's present in others. And the thing about accumulative inauthentic action is that with each action that takes us further from our cores, we tend to justify and prove to ourselves why it was the right decision. However, this same justification can be used as a checkpoint: when you notice yourself justifying an action to yourself, pause and ask yourself: *is this taking me further away from or closer towards myself?*

When you are far from your core self, it becomes easier to act in conflict with your highest good. And when this happens, you have guilt, low energy, low levels of motivation and a lack of enthusiasm for your life. It's virtually impossible to feel good when you are far away from yourself and what you know to be good for you.

If this resonates with you, I encourage you to take a moment to grab a pen and paper and try the following exercise:

- Write out what makes you feel your best, and some hobbies or interests you feel called to explore. Personally, time with my friends and loved ones, morning walks with a coffee and an evening read are what leave me feeling full and content.

Funnily enough, it's usually the simplest pleasures that mean the most.

• Take note of how much of your week revolves around what makes you feel your best. Work to build more of what you wrote down into the week ahead. Take a pause from reading and schedule it in your calendar *right now*.

## Latent past emotions

Another reason why you might experience a sense of heaviness out of the blue can be latent past emotions (past experiences you have not processed). I remember my mum telling me that worry was pointless because the real pain in life comes out of nowhere at 2pm on a Tuesday afternoon. What she meant was that the things that really shake us to our core come out of nowhere. Deaths, injuries, accidents and break-ups aren't planned in advance. There's no way to anticipate when they will happen or how. And when they do arrive in our lives, it can be so overwhelming that it's not possible to process them all at once.

When my father passed, it was too much for me to bear at the time. I was halfway through a year of travel with my boyfriend and was shellshocked when I heard the news. We flew to New Zealand for the funeral and continued on our trip after a short stint at home. I figured travelling again would be the best way to take my mind off what had happened. The pain of the experience was too heavy to carry all at once. The most I could hold was the funeral and saying goodbye, not the baggage of our relationship and processing his loss. My boyfriend and I travelled through Asia for five more months together, returning back to New York to set up a home base. On returning to New

York, I had every reason in the world to be elated with the state of my life. I had just finished travelling the world with the love of my life, secured a book deal for the very book you are reading now and had moved around the corner from my sister, her husband and my young nephew.

Despite everything on paper calling for me to feel appreciative and happy, I felt like I was drowning. I berated myself for not feeling good. I had a looming heaviness hanging over me, compounded by guilt for being ungrateful for the blessings in my life. I willed myself to feel better with all my might. But nothing would give.

We simply can't force ourselves to feel good.

It's like carrying bricks in our bag and asking our arms to feel less strained. We have to look at what we are carrying in order to put it down. After a couple of months of navigating in the dark, grasping at straws for what could be causing my mood to be so out of balance, it dawned on me. With the new-found stillness in my life, whatever I hadn't been able to process from the previous year would now be rising to the surface. I hadn't fully said goodbye to my father. I hadn't let myself really feel his death. I'd put it in a box and stored it away for some future time when I'd be better equipped to open it and look at the contents. It's natural to store things away for a time when we are better equipped to emotionally process them. But that process requires us to eventually take the time to review and clear out what may be sitting in our emotional garage.

What have you stored in boxes? What did you not have the full capacity to handle at the time? It could be from your childhood, your past relationships or losses. You may not feel ready to unbox the pain of your past and that's ok. If you do feel ready, but it is too overwhelming, I'd recommend seeking an additional layer of support – say, from a therapist or counsellor so you can work through it together.

## Lack of joy

And finally, another reason you can feel heavy in life is simply because you are not having enough experiences that bring you joy.

As I've said before, feeling good is our natural state of being. It is where you are most at home with yourself and others. Moments of explosive laughter, sharing a joke with your best friend, looking at someone you love with awe, noticing the beauty within ordinary moments . . . Joy is human. It feels light, airy and relaxed.

Building joy into your life is a precursor for feeling good more frequently. Joyful moments leave you feeling fluid and free. Similarly, a lack of joy is a sure way to feel the weight of the world on your shoulders. A moment of joy is an opportunity to put down whatever needs to be done and appreciate the beauty of the present moment for all that it is, and all that it is not. A moment to appreciate your life, instead of noticing all the reasons it doesn't measure up.

Take this moment to check in with yourself now: when was the last time you really laughed? When was the last time you were in awe? When was the last time you did something just for the delight of it?

There are many opportunities for joy that go unnoticed. See if you can direct your attention to pick up on moments that put a smile on your face. Pull a funny face at a small child to make them laugh. Notice how happy a dog looks walking in the park. Do something you want to do just for the pleasure of it.

When we act in alignment with our authentic selves, we walk our own paths. When we process latent emotion, we free ourselves from the pain of our pasts. When we move closer to joy, we move closer to our cores. Feeling good is our birthright. When we feel heavy and blue out of nowhere, this is an opportunity to reconnect with ourselves – an invitation to align with our authentic paths and purposes and to surrender what no longer needs to be carried.

Give yourself compassion as you navigate this time. You are doing a damned good job. Your willingness to sit and be with your uncomfortable feelings shows that you have the capacity to walk this path of healing. You are already well on your way and I'm proud of you.

## ✳ THREE REMINDERS WHILE NAVIGATING HEAVIER EMOTIONS

1. Our emotional state is like the ocean – instead of trying to control how you feel, let yourself ride the wave, knowing that even the wildest storms eventually calm.

2. We all have highs and lows. It's perfectly natural to be feeling the way you are and you are not alone.

3. Although joy may feel foreign right now, how could you build a little more light into each day? This could look like putting together a playlist of your favourite songs, taking a walk in the park or watching something that makes you laugh. Little moments can make major changes to your state.

Guiding principle

# You Can't Give from an Empty Cup

Saying yes to everyone else is one of the ways we often block ourselves from taking ownership of what we want in life and what we want to create. It's an easy story to fall into: '*I am too busy to work on that idea,*' '*I'll make more time next week to take care of myself.*' And on it goes, as we neglect what we need in favour of taking care of what seems more pressing.

There's a difference between naturally busy periods of life, and consciously and continuously putting too much on your plate. When you take on too much, it's common to skip over healthy habits you've intended to implement. But being 'too busy' is a poor excuse for not doing things that serve you and your greatest good. There is nothing more important than taking care of your health and wellbeing. It's what every other aspect of your life is built upon. Without good physical and emotional health, all areas of your life suffer.

Sacrificing your needs for the sake of meeting others' is a fast track to burnout. In fact, continuously saying yes to the needs of others when it means sacrificing your own often leads to resentment in the guise of being selfless. It serves no one. Over time, the people you are helping begin to feel like burdens and your giving comes from an empty cup. You end up robbing yourself of the delight of giving because it starts to feel like you are being taken from.

You cannot do it all, for everyone, all the time. And a great deal of peace will wash over you when you accept this truth because you will no longer hold yourself to an unattainable standard. All you can do is your best – and your best is reliant on how well you take care of yourself.

Taking care of yourself could look like the following:

• Taking ten minutes in the morning to centre before the day begins

• Not picking up your phone first thing in the morning

• Signing up for a yoga or movement class

• Holding yourself accountable to your goals

• Having clear boundaries between work and home life

• Going for a long walk

• Taking time to respond to a difficult situation

• Scheduling time to plan healthy meals for the week

Naturally there will be times where you are faced with a request or situation that requires you to reschedule and postpone the habits that fill your cup. Adaptability is important.

Sacrificing your needs
for the sake of meeting
others' is a fast track
to burnout.

Skipping a week or so of positive habits won't usually throw you off course, but missing them for a month or two might. The key is just to jump back in when you can, instead of continuing to put them off – there's no need to judge or guilt trip yourself. Because when you are in tune with what you need in order to feel your best, you have so much more energy to give to the world.

If you find yourself saying yes too often, or you lack the time for self-care, try the powerful exercise below and return to it regularly.

## ☀ FOUR QUESTIONS TO ASK YOURSELF BEORE YOU SAY YES

1. Do I innately want to do this?

2. Do I have the available capacity to say yes and still meet my own needs?

3. If there is a reward, is it worth the time and energy it will take?

4. Will doing this leave me feeling restored or depleted?

Guiding principle

# What You Don't Own Owns You

Like a lot of other light-workers in this world (*those of us who feel a deep calling to help others*), my desire to bring more love, light and joy into this life was born out of my experience of living in pain and darkness. As an extremely private person, this part of my past is something I've rarely talked about, even to those closest to me. So it's strange now to be sitting here on my couch, writing about it for you – a stranger. But in order for me to have the capacity to impart the teachings in this book, I must live by them in solidarity with you, so that you can see that maybe, in our shared experience, we aren't strangers, after all.

I was born into a tumultuous family life. My father was caught in the depths of a methamphetamine addiction and my mother struggled to raise four children by herself, plus a new baby. It wasn't always so crazy, though.

My father had a small business publishing school magazines when he and my mother met. When his publishing business fell apart, he took up temporary work as a mechanic, and when my mother became pregnant, then he began working with a property-development firm to better prepare for the arrival of his firstborn. He quickly excelled in his career, staying up late studying the building code and gaining a better understanding of the industry. As he continued to thrive at work, he separated from the firm and started working on developments on his own, gaining some notability in the city where I'm from. It became an all too sellable story of 'riches to rags' when drug addiction took hold of his life.

I came along years after the addiction began during a brief stint in which my mother had agreed to try to get the family back together again. In the chaos that surrounded my father – often hideous news articles and social drama – I was sent to live with my grandmother in the small southern hometown where my mum grew up. Months later, my grandmother explained it was too much for her and passed me on to a cousin who already had a young son. Within several months, she had become smitten, and my mother humbly agreed to my cousin adopting me in the hope that I would have a better life, removed from the drama of addiction.

But as fate would have it, my father heard the news and refused the idea. He contacted my cousin and bought flights for her to return me to his care.

I returned to Auckland to live with my father and connect back with my siblings at two years old. My father demanded that we live with him and that my mother stayed away for a year so that we could form some sort of relationship with him. Little did she know, much of that time was spent with nannies or just on our own when no one else was around.

Scattered in the memory of my past are times when I felt my whole body shake in terror as I heard my mother scream in fear of my father. Times when she swept me up in my blanket and put me in the back seat of the car just to drive and drive

It's only in fully accepting
your past that you can
fully accept all parts
of yourself.

AMBER LYON — YOU ARE A MAGNET

through the city until the sun came up. Times when we would go to visit my father wherever he was living at the time and I would see dirty mattresses on the ground, broken glass and makeshift curtains across the windows.

There were times in school when I was seven or eight when I would try to organise a playdate with friends and their parents wouldn't allow me to come over. Times when the gossiping whispers of those in class were audible just a few seats behind.

As a child, I internalised the shame of my father's choices. I saw his behaviour as a reflection of myself. I recognised that if people knew where I came from, it changed the way they saw me. I figured if I hid what was happening from others, they would be able to see *me* more clearly – not as the child of an addict, but just as me, Amber. I completely disowned the reality of my home life and it became my best-kept secret.

But the truth always comes to light. When we hide something from the world, we also hide the part of ourselves that has come from that experience. That separation and rejection of ourselves is where we leave room for shame to fester.

Eventually, my father was sent to prison, just as I was entering university. I saw my friends enjoying their new-found freedom and independence, while I felt paralysed, as an unbearable anxious weight triggered several panic attacks and a deep depression. With the reality of my family life plastered all over the national news, I could no longer hide from it. And as questions came from those around me wanting to understand why I had never shared what had happened, I quickly crumbled beneath them.

In denying one part of who we are, we deny all parts because we are inseparable from every experience we've ever had. Each and every one of them influences who we become. So when we hide parts of our past, we also hide parts of ourselves. It becomes impossible, then, to fully show up in the world as who we truly are.

It's only in fully accepting your past that you can fully accept all parts of yourself. The pain of unveiled secrets is simply the pain of others recognising something we refuse to. Like letting the light shine on skin not yet touched by the sun – it's fast to burn. It forces us to witness the rejected part of ourselves that longs to be accepted and integrated.

When you realise that what you carry the most shame around has, in fact, defined who you are today, you may be more willing to see it as the *critical part of your becoming that it is*. It is your pain that gives you purpose. It is the darkest nights that give you an appreciation of the morning light. The pain of your past has shaped you and what you stand for.

It's taken me a long time – perhaps until this moment, right now – to fully and wholeheartedly accept the pain of my past. To release the shame I have around what happened and what that might mean about who I am. In doing so, I've integrated the part of myself that came from that experience. Everything that has happened in my life has led me to this moment, sitting here right now, writing this book. I would not have had the heartfelt intention to help others feel better had I not gone through periods of my life when I didn't know how to break out of vicious, self-critical thoughts. I would not have had compassion for those in struggle if I had not seen the struggle in my own home. My pain has defined me. It has made me into the loving, kind, compassionate woman that I am. Hiding that part of myself was only hiding the beauty of alchemy. The magic of my own personal transformation.

Pain is my power – because it helps me to know more fully who I am.

Note: if you haven't shared your story before, seek out a professional or a trusted friend to open up to. There is something deeply healing about speaking aloud something you have kept hidden – you take back the power you've given it over your life.

## ✳ JOURNAL PROMPTS

I invite you to look at your own pain – parts of your life and your past that you may have disowned or rejected.

1. Looking back over your past experiences, which memories or relationships have left the greatest emotional imprint on you?

2. What have you learned about yourself through that experience? What skills did you gain?

3. Is there a way you could help others with the information you have?

Guiding principle

# Expectation Shapes Outcome

I first came across the law of expectation in *The Psychology of Achievement* by Brian Tracy. It was one of those 'aha' moments that changed my perception in one swift motion. I was in the middle of making myself oats for breakfast in my small apartment's kitchen, light streaming through the windows while listening to the audio of the book. As the conversation began, I forgot to stir the pot, burning my oats into an inedible mush.

The law of expectation is defined as whatever we believe will happen, usually does. Our expectations shape our outcomes because they determine how we act or behave. You and I both see an unknown and we each apply a different expectation. And it is our belief in that expectation that determines just how much time, energy and resources we are willing to invest into a positive outcome. If you look at a great unknown and expect disappointment or failure, you are going to invest a lot less than someone who expects good fortune and success. But how can we know what *may* happen? By referencing what we've experienced in the past.

The mind looks to reinforce where we've been, not where we wish to go. You may desire a promotion at work, but silently expect that someone else is more likely to get the position. So instead of putting your best foot forward and demonstrating your value, you are more likely to continue working at the same level of effort – accepting defeat before entering the race. The same goes for all goals and aspirations we have for our lives: the less we expect to achieve them, the more we fulfil that reality by not taking the action required. All of a sudden, what we expect to happen becomes our own self-fulfilling prophecy.

When we expect the worst of things, we prevent ourselves from showing up with the energy required to prove ourselves wrong. The mind constantly tries to ensure that you remain aligned with what you already know, even if what you know is in conflict with what you want.

We tend to believe in the voice that we hear in our minds and trust it as an accurate guide. But every thought that pops up, every expectation we place upon an experience, every assumption we make about others all come from a collection of our past experiences and beliefs. If we want a new experience, therefore, we have to leave room for the possibility of a different outcome. New expectations invite us to behave in different ways, and these actions take us to new places.

It may feel foreign, but foreign can be good. Foreign can lead us to new territories that we have never been to before. New results require new action – and new action requires thinking differently. It sounds simple, but this practice can truly change your life. Instead of believing the assumptions and expectations of the mind, see if you can build in space to question them. Pull them apart and see if you can look at the situation in question in a new way. By doing so, you will create a new way of being, affirming a life that aligns with what you want to create more than the reality of your past.

When we expect the worst of things, we prevent ourselves from showing up with the energy required to prove ourselves wrong.

AMBER LYON — YOU ARE A MAGNET

# ✳ REFLECTION

The next time you find yourself making assumptions or forming expectations of an outcome, pause and ask yourself:

1. Is there another way of looking at this?

2. If I expected the best of the situation, what action would I take next?

3. If there is a history of a certain outcome, what would I need to do in order to have a more positive outcome this time?

These questions create new thought patterns, those thought patterns lead to new actions and new actions lead to new outcomes.

Guiding principle

# Trusting in Higher Guidance

Back in December 2021, I was working in a property role with a small team in Auckland. I loved the people I worked with, but couldn't escape an inner knowing that I was making decisions that were safe, rather than aligned with who I was and what lit me up.

My sister, living in New York at the time with her husband, had recently had her first son, Elias. Because she was pregnant during the pandemic and the borders had been closed until the beginning of the year, I had not yet had the chance to meet my firstborn nephew. One quiet weekend afternoon, trusting an intuitive hit to meditate, I lay on my bed and had a clear directive: go to New York.

It didn't make sense, to say the least. Flights were expensive, I was knee deep in a new project at work and New Zealand's borders were still fluctuating between open and closed, leaving the possibility of being unable to return home. But something quietly called for me to walk forward – that feeling when something feels right in your bones, yet unreasonable to the mind. My intuitive guidance was giving me directions that did not make sense, but I knew I had to follow them to find out where they led.

Within a few weeks I had booked tickets, told my elated sister I was coming and had organised a short time off from work. When I got to New York, the feeling of meeting my nephew – seeing his precious new face and wise eyes – made it all worthwhile. And spending time with my sister and supporting her in this new stage of life was an experience I will be forever grateful for.

A week into my trip, New Zealand announced that they were shutting their borders once again, leaving me stranded in the city. I berated myself, my logical mind jumping on the opportunity to reinforce itself and the doubts I'd had before booking my trip. But there was more to come to justify my inner calling.

A few years prior, I had met a guy in New York who I had connected with. At a dinner organised by mutual friends, we happened to sit next to each other and ended up laughing the night away together. I remember thinking to myself I had never smiled more in my life. With our respective schedules and the small issue of not living in the same country, we never had the chance to explore more than a friendship, but we kept in touch over the years.

Fast forward to February 2022, and there we were, back in New York, having a drink to catch up on the years gone by and what was happening in our lives. He told me about a year-long solo trip he was planning. He was going to travel the world, starting in South America, exploring the Amazon rainforest, moving on to Africa, Europe, Southeast Asia and finishing in the Pacific. I was intrigued – '*What an adventure!*'

Over the next few weeks, we continued to spend time together. There was a sense that I was participating in something beyond my control. Each time we met up would be spent laughing and chatting, holding the type of magic feeling that exists beyond the realm of the logical mind. Something that felt not quite understood. The hints of what could be when we'd first met now solidified into a connection I had never felt before in my life. A sense of home shared with someone else.

With the borders still closed back home, I organised a visa for London and prepared to move to a new city. In the wave of change outside of my control, my only choice was to make the best of the situation and see the move as a new adventure of my own.

As the date of Jon's departure approached, I couldn't help but feel a sense of disappointment at the thought of letting go of a connection that had shown me what was possible in a relationship. One that broke the mould of what I thought I wanted for myself. Despite the disappointment, I retained a quiet knowing. If we were meant to explore more together, then it would happen in the future. I could not control the details, but I could control how I showed up to the experience. I wanted to focus on the time we still had together and on enjoying that, rather than what was going to happen next.

At our last dinner together, we laughed and chatted about the adventures to come over wine and pasta. In a moment between moments, Jon said he had a proposition for me: why not come? To not explore what we had between us – something neither of us yet fully understood – would be an uncertainty he could not live with.

Certainly, it was a crossroads: to follow the path that I thought made sense or to trust one that felt right in my bones but terrified me beyond imagination. The sheer extent of the uncertainty felt like a great abyss before me. Looking into his

# What may not make sense now is leading you to what will in time.

eyes, though, my whole being said yes before I'd had the chance to open my mouth. In the moment, I was sure; it was simultaneously the right decision and the one that made least sense to my logical mind.

In the days to come, I faced the doubts and uncertainty of those around me about my choice. In the noise of it all, I questioned myself and my innate knowing. It felt irresponsible, unrealistic, unlikely that any good would come from such a spur-of-the-moment change in course. But how could I know if I did not try? What true harm could come from giving something new a go?

For the first time in my life, I let go of my need to know how something would go. I released my control and expectations of what might happen next and leaned into a stillness that held me through the fears that ran through my mind. I still recall the feeling of boarding my flight to meet him in Costa Rica, the first destination in what may or may not have been many more to come. *One day at a time*, I repeated to myself whenever the fears and doubts started to rise. *If I remain present with just each day and trust myself to pivot if it no longer feels right, everything will be ok.*

I remember the electric jitters in my body as I landed and waited to clear customs. I remember the heavy pounding of my heart as I neared the arrivals hall. I remember the delight as we saw each other once again and the wave of peace that washed over me. And I remember the next ten months we spent travelling together, falling more and more in love as we explored the world and our connection.

It was a string of decisions that did not make sense but felt right in my bones. A slew of experiences that led me to a daily encounter with joy, rather than an idealised destination. That's all magnetism truly is: listening to our intuitive guidance and what feels right in the moment, even if that choice may not make sense to anyone else.

When we trust that our intuitive insights come from higher guidance, it makes it easier to act on them, each little clue unveiling the journey moment by moment. When we trust what feels right and true in this moment, we can trust that we are always on the right track. What may not make sense now is leading you to what will in time.

## ✳ TRUSTING IN YOUR OWN HIGHER GUIDANCE

1. Bring to mind a situation you are finding difficult to navigate at the moment.

2. In a quiet space where you won't be interrupted, sit comfortably and close your eyes.

3. Place your hand on your heart and meditate on the question: 'What do I need to know to navigate this situation with ease?'

4. When you have finished your meditation, journal any insights that came through.

Guiding principle

# You Decide What's Realistic

The word 'realistic' has always really bothered me. Any time I'd get inspired and think big about the possibilities of my life, I'd be met by voices around me reminding me to be *realistic* about my goals.

But what does 'realistic' really mean? *To be sensible about what can be achieved?* To be sensible about the vision you have for your life is to restrict what is possible for you. Your dreams and visions are not supposed to be sensible – they are supposed to *inspire you*. To be so alluring that they pull you into the great unknown.

Just as we are magnetic, the vision we have for our lives also magnetically pulls us towards it. The stronger the vision, the stronger your sensation to move forward will be. If your dream is realistic, you are invited to dream bigger. There is no boundary of what's within reach to everyone. What is 'realistic' is set by each of us personally, defined by our own unique set of experiences, desires and beliefs. What's realistic to someone else is a reflection of what *they* believe is possible in life, but that doesn't have to be your truth.

# The only person your goals have to be realistic for is your future self.

What is realistic to you is the dream you have in your heart and where you feel called to go.

The only person your goals have to be realistic for is your future self. Because even you will doubt the possibility of what your life could be until you see it before you. But you've got to trust in the vision you have more than the circumstances in front of you. There's always going to be a gap between where you are and what you are working towards, but this gap is not a signal that your dreams are unrealistic; rather, it is an invitation to consistently keep moving towards them. Let the discomfort of that distance be your motivation to make your dream your reality. The only way to prove to yourself what's possible is to put one foot after another and see where you end up.

It would not be in your heart if it was not your path to walk.

## ✳ IF SOMEONE IS TELLING YOU TO BE 'REALISTIC' WITH YOUR DREAMS

1. Remember that what they are really telling you is that what you want for yourself is out of *their* realm of possibility.

2. If it's in your heart, and you feel called to fulfil something that may fall outside the box of what you've always done, it is your *destiny to fulfil* that calling.

3. You are the only person who gets to decide what's possible for your life.

Guiding principle

# Go At Your Own Speed

Everyone has their own tempo – a natural pace for navigating life that feels most comfortable for them. But in a world where things always seem to be behind schedule, there's a tendency to feel the pressure to accelerate. For short bursts, this doesn't do much damage. But when you continuously push yourself beyond your capacity, you'll eventually have to stop and catch your breath. Oftentimes, if you don't stop, your body will stop you through exhaustion, burnout or sickness.

Succumbing to the pressure for things to be done as quickly as possible not only burns you out in terms of energy, but also deprives you of creative exploration – something that could, given the opportunity, lead to better solutions and outcomes in the long term. Sometimes the most productive thing you can do in your day is to take a break and reset your system. When you slow down and find your own natural rhythm, your creative energy will start to flow effortlessly. A short walk can present solutions that staring at a screen or an empty piece of paper simply cannot. Taking time to find your natural rhythm is key to tapping into your flow state.

The same goes for your interpersonal relationships. There are no specific requirements that you *have to* meet. Your needs will be different to others' and therefore you may need more or less time with the people you care about. If you identify as someone that needs a lot of downtime alone to feel recharged (introverted), your social schedule may not look as full as that of someone who feels energised by being around others (extroverted). Being magnetic means that you understand yourself well enough to know you have your own unique needs. An introvert forcing themselves to constantly be social is not conducive to them embodying their highest self. Similarly, an extrovert who forces themselves to spend a lot of time alone does not allow themselves to shine and recharge in the ways they so authentically need. The key is to take the time to check in and ask yourself : what's the optimum amount of social time I need each week to feel my best?

Sometimes you need a break, while other times you realise you need to dive in more fully. But you always intuitively know what's best for *you* when you take the time to check in.

## ☀ TAKING AN OPPORTUNITY TO SLOW DOWN

1. A short breathwork exercise or a five-minute meditation around lunch can completely transform the second half of your day.

2. Although it can feel like 'there's no time', the little self-care pockets you build into the day create a ripple effect on how you show up to every task that follows.

3.  If meditation is not for you, try a short walk outside, ideally at a park.

Taking time to find your natural rhythm is key to tapping into your flow state.

Guiding principle

# When the Wave Crashes, Let It Crash

Don't waste your energy trying to fight it. Your resistance only adds to the pressure of the water pushing down. Instead, lean into it. Flow with wherever it takes you. Go deeper. Stay curious and open-minded. Be kind to yourself as you learn to breathe underwater. It *will* pass and, before long, you will feel lighter and the day before you will start to colour again. Stay patient. This moment, over time, will come to be a distant blur in what has evolved into a rich and beautiful life.

## ✳ FOUR LOVING REMINDERS

1. Sometimes you just have to get through; and getting through is more than enough.

2. Don't add extra pressure on yourself to fight what you are feeling. When you accept it, it naturally becomes lighter.

Stay patient. This moment, over time, will come to be a distant blur in what has evolved into a rich and beautiful life.

3. You are not alone. Almost every person you pass on the street has, at one point or another, felt how you are feeling right now.

4. Life is a rollercoaster. Just as it has its ups, there are always going to be downs. It's all part of the ride.

Guiding principle

# Forgiveness Will Set You Free

We've each had our own fair share of experiences with people who did not have the capacity to love us in ways that we needed them to. This disappointment can create deep emotional wounds – the type that ache long after the experience in question has passed.

All pain calls for healing, *but it's impossible to fully heal when you are still wishing things had been different.* The anger you hold for what has happened in your past acts like a concrete block tied to your feet as you try to swim. Even as you move forward in your life, whatever past pain you are holding is carried into your future relationships. We each have our own emotional baggage we may be carrying – a collection of hurt that still feels tender to the touch. After years of walking around holding what has happened on our backs, the weight eventually takes a toll on our inner being.

Often, an inability to forgive others for their choices manifests as a need to make perfect choices in our own life. It's a mechanism that quickly leads to walking an inauthentic path. How often have you behaved in a certain way to prove a point to someone else? Perhaps an attempt to make someone regret the hurt they inflicted on you? When you create from this place, you give away your power. All your energy and attention are fixated on your past, rather than being channelled into creating your future.

Sometimes the people we love don't have the capacity to give us what we need or can't love us in the way we wish they could. As painful as being let down can be, when we hold anger and resentment towards another, we truly only punish ourselves. In fact, those latent feelings keep our emotional wounds open. The key to healing lies in realising that we cannot change the past; all we can do is make peace with it. This does not mean continuing to accept less than we deserve or letting go of accountability from those who hurt us, but it's about knowing that our power lies in surrendering what we cannot change. Instead of wishing things were different, or that someone could have been the person we needed, we accept what is.

Your acceptance is your reclamation of power. It's knowing you will not stand to be treated the same way again. Yes, things could have been better, and it's terribly painful to have someone you love let you down, but by not letting it go, you let yourself down. You deserve to be free of your past. And when you accept circumstances and people as they are, you reclaim your power to create something different.

The act of forgiving is never for the benefit of the one who hurt you, but for yourself. So that you can live your life without your past experiences weighing you down. Forgiving does not mean allowing – just *releasing*. Releasing what happened so that you can be fully present with your life now. Healing is forgiving the pain of your past, knowing it has shaped you into who you are today. And forgiveness is so that you can create from a place

of being unencumbered, so your past does not dictate the decisions you make today. It's letting go of the need for things to be
any way other than how they are, knowing that your history is
not your future. It's having understanding and compassion for
the imperfections of others and setting boundaries so that it
does not happen again.

Forgive – so that you can open fully to this moment now.

 ## EXERCISE IN FORGIVENESS

1. Think of someone who hurt you in the past and towards
   whom you may still harbour some pain or resentment.
   Are there some unspoken words in your heart?

2. Take a pen and paper and write this person a letter,
   letting them know how you feel. Be as honest and
   vulnerable as possible.

3. When you have finished, burn this letter (carefully, in
   a space where it is safe to do so) or rip it up and throw
   it away.

4. Perhaps there are words you still wish to share if it is
   possible/safe to do so? Otherwise, the act of writing and
   destroying this letter acts as an emotional release.

Healing is forgiving the
pain of your past, knowing
it has shaped you into
who you are today.

Guiding principle

# Celebrate What You Like about Yourself

People will always have an opinion about you and what you do. Instead of focusing on how you can convince others of your value, see if you can instead focus on what it is you truly value about yourself.

When you embrace this shift and own whatever it is that lights you up and brings you joy, the world will adjust accordingly. Others will still have their opinions, but you will be so grounded in yourself that these will wash over you like rain across trees. When you learn to like yourself, you will radiate that energy into every space you enter, freeing yourself to focus on following your authentic path and living in alignment with it, while inspiring others to do the same.

When you learn to like yourself, you will radiate that energy into every space you enter.

# ✳ HOW TO CULTIVATE INNER RADIANCE

1. For the week ahead, take a few moments in the morning while brushing your teeth to think of one thing you like about yourself. It can be a characteristic or a physical trait, but it has to feel true.

2. Before a social situation or event you feel nervous about, place your hand on your heart and remind yourself of all those things. This will connect you back into your magnetic self and this energy will radiate from you.

Guiding principle

# You Are Capable of Change

There is no one else who mysteriously enters our lives and sets in motion the actions necessary to create the lives we dream of. If anyone is going to change your life, it's you.

When you surrender the idea that someone else is going to save the day, you take back your power to save it yourself. You are capable of change at any moment. If what you've created so far no longer feels good, you can shift your focus, energy and actions to bring about a new reality.

If what you've created so far no longer feels good, you can shift your focus, energy and actions to bring about a new reality.

AMBER LYON — YOU ARE A MAGNET

# ✳ SEVEN LIFE-CHANGING REMINDERS

1. Invest in people who have the capacity and willingness to invest in you, too.

2. Forgive others – not for their peace of mind but for your own.

3. Difficult times shaped you into who you are today.

4. Your intuition is always speaking to you.

5. Know that every person, situation and experience is an opportunity to grow.

6. Dreams are achieved by making peace with your doubts and walking forward anyway.

7. When you are at peace with yourself, you radiate a magnetic energy.

# PART THREE

# Guiding Principles for the Magnetic Mindset

# Pain Will Push You until Vision Pulls

Feeling stuck, constantly reflecting on past experiences or feeling the sensation of not going anywhere, often come as a result of lacking a clear vision for what's next. If we are not working towards something, it's impossible not to relive our pasts and feel stuck in our circumstances – even if we find ourselves in a place we previously prayed to reach.

Pain pushing you forward can look like a toxic relationship ending, an unfulfilling job letting you go or simply not knowing what you want. These painful changes (many of which we explored in Part Two: Cultivating Courage) are all signals that life is trying to push you into the next chapter of your life. Although all these experiences serve our growth, they certainly don't feel pleasant.

But your life is always serving your highest purpose. No pain comes without the intention to grow us or encourage us to reflect on what it is we truly want for the next season of our lives. Sometimes change and the pain of life can be the *exact catalyst* we need to make new decisions – to set new expectations of ourselves.

In order to feel motivated to move forward, we need something inspiring enough to work towards. Setting a vision for our lives, or clear goals sort of acts like a rope to hold onto to keep us from falling back into old habits and patterns of behaviour. In fact, when we have clarity on what we are trying to create, each little step we take towards that place contributes to our sense of progress and self esteem. When it comes to setting your own vision for this next chapter in life, know that it does not have to revolve around external achievements. In fact, there have been many times when I've simply worked towards a calmer state of being or on deepening my relationships. Just trust whatever feels most pressing and inspiring to you in this moment.

If you have been feeling stagnant or stuck in your past, I invite you to reflect on whether you have a clear vision for what you are working towards. If you do not, take some time now to do the vision-setting exercise that follows.

When we have clarity on what
we are trying to create, each little
step we take towards that place
contributes to our sense
of progress and self-esteem.

AMBER LYON — YOU ARE A MAGNET

# ✳ VISION SETTING

Explore the following questions in your journal:

1. What would get me out of bed every morning?

2. What have I always dreamed of doing, or being a part of?

3. If I could travel into the future, what would I look back on and regret not doing?

4. If I knew I would succeed, what would I pursue?

5. What is it that I am most craving in my life currently?

Go on to Pinterest or find some magazines and put together some visuals that inspire you. Pick out images that light you up and reflect the responses of your journal reflections above. These are visual references for what you want the next chapter of your life to look like. Be open and don't limit yourself to what you think is possible or within reach.

Give this next chapter a name or title. For example, 'The season of love' or 'The embodiment of success'. Get creative and trust whatever intuitively comes up for you.

Guiding principle

# It's Never Too Late to Start

What better moment to start creating the life you dream of than this one right now?

Perhaps you'll have more resources, skills and time in the future, but *perhaps not*. The idea that you are not ready is an illusion. The truth is you are ready when you decide you are. In fact your very desire for something is an indication that you are being called forward. The question is: will you take the first step?

It's easy to find evidence to remain where we are. Our self-critic is quick to voice why we're not equipped for what we want. But I'd like you to consider that: the only resistance between where you are and where you'd like to be is your belief in your thoughts of self-doubt. *What if they weren't true?*

There's unlikely to be a point in time when you feel totally ready for what you want. The trick is to walk forward anyway. Knowing that the only way to figure it out lies in doing it. You may trip, fall and face setbacks along the way, but it's all part of the experience. This is the adventure of your life. Will you set sail or wonder about a different life from the shore?

181

Desire is all you need to get started. The tools and resources will continue to emerge as you make the most of what you already have at your disposal. You don't have to be the best to start, but you do have to start to be the best.

## ✳ FOUR PROMPTS FOR WHEN YOU DON'T FEEL READY

1. What have you been telling yourself that you 'can't' do lately?

2. Could you write out a list of reasons why you could?

3. Write out all the positive things that could come from taking action towards a dream or goal.

4. You may never feel ready for what you truly desire, but do not let that hold you back from taking action.

This is the adventure of your life. Will you set sail or wonder about a different life from the shore?

AMBER LYON — YOU ARE A MAGNET

Guiding principle

# Be Mindful of Your Self-Talk

We are always in a silent conversation with ourselves – an endless stream of dialogue in our minds either building us up or breaking us down. Such an important part of shifting our mindsets and tapping into a magnetic state is becoming more aware of the way we speak *to* ourselves *about* ourselves.

Our inner dialogue delicately shapes whether we feel empowered or disempowered in any given situation. We speak to ourselves more than anyone else on the planet, so it's important to be mindful of what we are saying. Statements that follow 'I' or 'I am' are so powerful because they define how we see ourselves. When you find yourself in challenging circumstances and ruminate on thoughts like 'I'll never be able to do this,' 'I am not smart enough,' or 'Why does this always happen to me?' It's natural to feel demotivated and a victim of the situation. When we listen to negative self talk, we drain our energy. Eventually even the simplest tasks become opportunities to feel discouraged.

Our self-talk can either affirm old limiting beliefs or can be used to introduce new dialogue that affirms new beliefs.

Practising *positive* self-talk is key to correcting the self-image distortions you may have come to believe about yourself.

Personally, when I notice my self-talk is leaning heavily towards judgment or continuously landing on disempowering conclusions, it's a clear signal that I need to reintroduce my affirmations.

Positive affirmations are empowering statements about yourself and your life. They introduce new, expansive beliefs that boost confidence, motivation and the ability to extend self-compassion. In using affirmations, we aren't trying to brush over deeper emotions that may need processing or fake a mood when it feels inauthentic; rather, we are introducing a counter-balance to our destructive thoughts. And, in doing so, we help reinforce new beliefs. Then, the more we use and repeat them, the more we internalise the words until, over time, they become a part of our self-identity.

Although positive affirmations aren't for everyone, they're a powerful tool in shifting your mindset on a daily basis. I find myself returning to them whenever I'm feeling low or lacking confidence. I've included some of my favourite daily affirmations on the following page. You can speak them out loud or say them in your mind. Use them when you find yourself in a challenging situation and notice if you feel more empowered and confident afterwards.

You speak to yourself more than anyone else on the planet, so it's important to be mindful of what you are saying.

AMBER LYON — YOU ARE A MAGNET

# ✳ FIVE MAGNETIC AFFIRMATIONS

1. 'I can do hard things.'

2. 'I am intelligent and capable of finding solutions,
   no matter the problem.'

3. 'I am always learning and growing.'

4. 'I am loved; it is safe for me to share and receive love
   with others.'

5. 'I trust myself and my life. This is all serving my
   highest good.'

Guiding principle

# Getting Clear on Your Values

Our values are what we believe to be the most important parts of life. You can imagine, then, that when we live our lives out of sync with them, it would be natural to feel off centre. The problem is, so many of us aren't living in alignment with our values simply because we lack clarity on what they are, or we've been living according to someone else's.

So what are values? Values can be defined as the core principles we strive for. They are standards that we set for ourselves and the world around us on what is right, wrong and fair. They determine what we pursue and what we avoid in life, influencing how we behave and interact with the world around us. Our dream life is often simply an expression of all of our values being present in our world. Often, the sensations of being lost and disconnected, as we discussed earlier, come as a result of not having clarity on what's truly important to us in life.

Knowing yourself and what's important to you is the embodiment of magnetism.

Many of the values we hold reflect those most common among our parental figures and friends. But part of taking ownership of our lives involves reflecting on whether we fundamentally share those values or have just adopted them by default. Many of my clients raised in strict religious homes, for example, have found that their values are very different to those of their parents, while others share the same values, but within a different hierarchy – that is the order of importance to them. It makes sense for the hierarchy to be different because each of us have our own unique blueprint for what's important in life.

Getting clear on your values allows you to create a life that accurately reflects what's truly important *to you*. When you have this clarity, it's much easier to create an aligned life because you have such insight into what fits in with your values – and what doesn't. Put simply, living in alignment with your values is the fastest way to bring fulfilment and a sense of purpose back into your daily life.

The key here is to embed your values into the routine of each day. That way, every day contributes to feeling connected with your greater meaning.

I've included one of my favourite exercises shared with clients on the following pages, so that you too can gain clarity on what's most important to you. This is single-handedly the most important tool I've used to increase my general satisfaction and contentment in life.

# ✳ VALUE CLARITY EXERCISE

Grab a journal or pen and paper and work through the following prompts:

1. What things in life bring you the most satisfaction?

2. What would you spend your time doing if you were retired or financially free?

3. What is really important to you to do daily?

4. What makes you feel your best?

Here are a few examples of what you might include:
   Constantly learning and growing, moving your body and feeling physically strong, great relationships, feeling loved and loving others, fulfilling work that makes a positive impact on the world, writing regularly, safe home base; somewhere that feels like an oasis and the ability to be your own boss and set your own schedule

Next, read through the following values, then go back through the list you wrote above and pick the value that best captures the core of what you've written. You are welcome to use a value that's not listed below – these are just suggestions:
   **Freedom, self-improvement, spontaneity, connection, security, self-care, physical health, contribution, creativity, beauty, exploration, independence and play.**

Knowing yourself and
what's important to you
is the embodiment of
magnetism.

For example:

- Constantly learning and growing = **SELF-IMPROVEMENT**

- Moving your body and feeling physically strong = **SELF-IMPROVEMENT**

- Great relationships, feeling loved and loving others = **CONNECTION**

- Fulfilling work that makes a positive impact on the world = **CONTRIBUTION**

- Writing regularly = **CREATIVITY**

- A safe home base; somewhere that feels like an oasis = **SECURITY**

- The ability to be my own boss and set my own schedule = **FREEDOM**

Finally, see which, if any, of the values has shown up more than once and write a new list – one that will reflect your unique values, ordering them from 1 to 4, starting with the one/s that appear most frequently on your original list.

For example:
1. Self-improvement
2. Connection
3. Contribution
4. Freedom

**Reflection**

If you've noticed through this exercise that how you spend your time does not reflect the values now in front of you, this is the perfect opportunity to recalibrate. Build a few things into your schedule this week that better reflect your new value hierarchy. For example: if you value physical health, but that's not reflected in how you spend your time, it's very powerful to prioritise some movement into your week.

Guiding principle

# Tapping into Your Magnetic Self

We so seldom stop and ask ourselves: is my way of being in the world achieving the results that I seek? We become so wedded to our habitual way of thinking and behaving that it can feel strange to consider showing up in a different way. But, ultimately, who you show up as today is just a collection of decisions made by a past version of yourself. If you want to create something new or different, you are going to have to make new decisions.

Being magnetic is simply creating an authentic vision for who you want to be in the world (one that is in tune with your true self and values) and showing up as that person. While some call this your highest self, I've always loved referring to it as your most 'magnetic self'. It's not a character or role to play or trying to be like anyone else, but who you are beneath the limiting beliefs that have convinced you otherwise. You were born to take up space in the world – to embody your energy in its fullest capacity. But it's also absolutely natural that you do not feel that way right now.

We are taught to doubt ourselves. To play small. To be sensible and realistic about our goals in life. This is your invitation in this moment to let all that go. To be radically open-minded about what's possible and to let yourself play with the idea you can show up in a new way.

Your magnetic self represents who you would effortlessly show up as if you had never collected any doubt in your potential. Your greater goal, and through each principle in this book, is to connect with this version of yourself. It's not some static state of being, but an adaptable one that evolves as you grow and your desires change. The magnetic self of your twenties is going to be very different to that of your thirties, forties or fifties because what you want in life changes over time. As you reach one goal, you are invited to set another and so on.

## ✳ PART 1: UNCOVERING YOUR MAGNETIC SELF

1. I'd like you to reflect on the vision you have for this next chapter of your life

2. When you think of the best possible outcome for this chapter — what does that look like? Physically where are you? Who are you surrounded by? What have you achieved?

3. Now take a moment to think about the version of yourself that exists in this best-case scenario — what habits and characteristics would this version of yourself have?

This is your magnetic self.

Uncovering the magnetic self means simply deciphering what traits and characteristics would be required to embody our visions. When we think of manifesting, we usually consider what we'd like to attract into our lives. We tend to hyperfixate on the details of what we are calling in, rather than what's far more important: how we will feel in that experience and how we think it will change us.

External desires are simply invitations to catalyse something within us. It's not so much about where we want to go, but who we become on the way there. The art of magnetism is bringing our visions into the present moment by showing up as our magnetic selves today.

When we radiate this new energy, our visions effortlessly pull towards us and wonderful synchronicities enter our lives. And because what we want in life constantly evolves as we grow, it's important to regularly check in with ourselves, setting new visions and connecting with different iterations of our most magnetic selves.

It's not so much
about where we want to go,
but who we become on
the way there.

# ✳ PART 2: TAPPING INTO YOUR MAGNETIC SELF

1. Bring to mind the vision you summoned up in Part 1 of this exercise, on the previous pages.

2. What traits, characteristics and habits do you have in this vision? (This is your magnetic self.) Write them out now.

3. How could you cultivate more of those characteristics today?

4. What habits of your magnetic self could you schedule into this coming week?

Guiding principle

# Create Your Own Glimmers

Going about their day, the average person has between 12,000 and 60,000 thoughts (I've certainly felt on the higher end of that spectrum in the past). Interestingly, almost 95 per cent of those thoughts are simply the same recycled ones as the day before.

As we explored in Part One, feelings trigger thoughts, thoughts trigger actions and our actions determine outcomes. So it makes sense that the recycled thoughts of yesterday set in motion a very similar self today. But what triggers our feelings to set that in motion in the first place? Answer: cues from our environment.

Environmental cues are triggers from our physical world that spark certain thoughts to follow. At surface value, the way we organise our rooms or where certain items are placed in our kitchen may seem insignificant, but these things end up having an enormous impact on our thoughts and behaviour. For example, when you wake up in the morning and the room is cluttered or messy, that sight is a cue for certain thoughts to follow: 'I still haven't done the washing,' 'I wish someone would help me clean up more,' etc. Likewise, when we see clean, folded gym clothes on waking up in the morning, this visual gives us a cue to think or behave in a different way, actually increasing the likelihood that we will put on those clothes and head to the gym. When it comes to our kitchen, the placement of healthy food options versus less healthy snacks has a major influence over what we reach for (one thing we know for sure: out of sight, out of mind). Our behaviour is influenced by what our environment makes most convenient (or inconvenient – say, removing unhealthy snacks from our home altogether).

Because our routines and habits tend to look similar day to day, our environmental cues trigger the same ways of thinking and feeling. No wonder, then, that when we try to introduce a mindset change within the same environment, it's so easy to slip back into old patterns. It's less that we don't have the will-power, and more that we are setting ourselves up to fail by not introducing a *positive trigger* for that new behaviour.

In the work I do with private clients, we create new environmental cues that reinforce a new way of being to align with their goals, values and magnetic selves. Triggering new thoughts requires new triggers or, in other words, we have to create opportunities to think in a new way. And we can do this by adding *glimmers* into our day.

I first came across the word glimmers on Instagram in a post by a friend and therapist Helen Marie, although it was first coined by Deb Dana in in her book *The Polyvagal Theory in Therapy*. Helen described glimmers as the opposite of triggers – little moments that spark joy and an inner calm. I immediately lit up when I heard the term because it was the first time I had heard a name for what I had been working with clients to build into their days – moments of joy that would trigger new thought cycles.

All too often, what blocks us from showing up in a new way is just our automatic responses to our environment. Nothing changes if nothing changes. The ability to show up in new ways requires us to build in more glimmers, and to reduce the negative triggers.

## ✳ SETTING IN MOTION NEW THOUGHTS

Today, I'd like your focus to be on completing the following guided exercise that outlines how you can build more glimmers and reduce negative triggers in your own life.

### Creating glimmers

1. Create an album on your phone of photos that feel like your magnetic self. Include pictures of yourself during a period when you felt particularly confident or radiant. Also, add anything that reminds you of positive experiences of embodying your truest self – text messages of appreciation from friends, or moments where you felt your strongest. Include inspirational pictures of others that embody traits you are working to own or want to cultivate. Name this album 'Glimmers' and return to it throughout the week to remind yourself of your innate magnetism.

2. Create a new music playlist that reflects your highest self. This is just a collection of songs that make you feel your best – capable of taking on the world. Put this on as you

# Nothing changes if nothing changes.

get ready for the day, or while you travel to work in the morning.

3. Add one thing to your bedroom that feels authentic to you. Perhaps it's a piece of art, flowers or simply reorganising the space to make it feel clearer and cleaner. Whatever you do, make sure that it makes the space feel more reflective of you and your magnetic self

## Reducing negative triggers

1. Do a full social media cleanse. Unfollow accounts that make you feel 'less than' or trigger you. You owe no explanations or apologies.

2. Set a time limit for using social media apps that you feel are draining your free time or damaging your self image.

3. Go through your wardrobe and get rid of things you haven't worn in the past one to two years by donating them to charity or selling them online. (It feels so good to let go of things that no longer reflect who you are.)

Guiding principle

# Making Magnetic Decisions

Getting clear on what decision to make requires becoming still. So still that sound itself begins to slow, and in the cracks between the noise of the world and the mind, our own insights begin to emerge. As we explored in previous principles, you can connect with your intuitive guidance through the practices of meditation, breathwork, journaling or sitting quietly with yourself. Sometimes all it takes is just being present with where you are. Simply spending time with yourself cultivates self-trust, allowing your guidance system to feel safe to pass on insights that will help make the best decision a little clearer.

Sometimes the insights that come through are confronting: a gut feeling that we no longer connect with a friend or a romantic partner in the same way as before; an intuitive knowing that we are in the wrong job for our skills and interests. Our intuitive guidance lets us know where to go, regardless of the circumstances we may have to face to get there.

Perhaps the decision that you feel called to make has consequences for someone you care about, or you feel it would disappoint someone. As difficult as these choices are, they are nowhere near as painful as staying off course from your authentic path.

It's possible to feel two things at once: a deep calling for change and a resistance or guilt about the actions required to make that change. As challenging as it can be to change our minds, let someone down or disappoint someone, if something no longer adds value to our lives or no longer feels aligned, it is our total responsibility to choose differently. If you are holding yourself accountable to the decisions of a past version of yourself that no longer make you happy, it is time to change course. Making magnetic decisions is really about being clear on who you are and *what's important to you*. Perhaps that means choosing to spend less time with someone that no longer feels good to be around. Or it may look like reorganizing your schedule to make room for daily movement. You will have your own guidance on what the next best step is – but you've got to create space to hear it.

Seeking clarity on which decision to make requires getting quiet enough to hear how you truly feel about what's going on. We each have an enormous well of insights and guidance available to us when we create space to hear them. And from this space, you will always hear what you need to hear. *It may not be what you want to hear*, but your intuitive insights are always guiding you to your highest path. Try to remember that what feels painful in the immediate often paves the way for the best that's yet to come. No one will thank you for living a life that did not feel right in your bones.

Your decisions need to first and foremost serve your wellbeing. Your future self will thank you for the difficult decisions you made today.

 EXERCISE FOR CLARITY

1. Bring to mind what you are trying to make a
   decision about.

2. Close your eyes and focus on your breathing.

3. Once you feel settled and your breathing is slow, deep
   and calm, affirm: 'I already have awareness on the best
   and highest solution for all. I allow this guidance to come
   forward now.'

4. Sit for a few moments and see what insights come forward
   when you create space for them.

If something no longer
adds value to our lives or
no longer feels aligned, it is
our total responsibility to
choose differently.

AMBER LYON — YOU ARE A MAGNET

Guiding principle

# There Is Always Another Route

Imagine you've set out on a road trip with a full tank of petrol. Unbeknown to you, there's a roadblock on the way to where you're trying to go. With half a tank of petrol left, you are faced with a choice: to try and force the road blockers to let you through (burning through your remaining gas as you wait) or to find another route to your destination. Which of these sounds better to you?

This situation mirrors the delays, setbacks and disappointments we face when we are trying to work towards something. Whether it be a state of mind, a goal or a destination, we'd like to arrive there as soon as possible, so it's natural to feel jarred by not being able to do so. But sitting in front of a setback and trying to forcefully shift it into something else tends to exhaust our precious energy, putting us into a frustrated state of mind.

When we remain adaptable – meaning we are open to finding a new way to get where we're trying to go – we release the pressure we've placed on the world to meet our expectations and timelines. All of a sudden, we don't feel like we're in as much of a rush because we understand that we are always on time for our own lives. This perspective and energetic state opens us up to the idea that an alternative route may have its own blessings.

Detours can be one of the most unappreciated gifts of life. Answered prayers often come in the form of delays and setbacks, making them difficult to recognise. If you stay open to the way life is redirecting your path, you will be able to see how this circumstance is nudging you in a new direction. Trust that it is all serving a purpose in your authentic path. The very frustration you feel now is triggering a new way forward.

The world doesn't work to your timelines or perfectly laid plans. Trying to force *your way* over *life's way* is mentally exhausting. So use your energy for what's important – that is, moving forward in the journey. Let yourself appreciate the views along a route you may not have seen before.

## ※ FOUR REMINDERS FOR WHEN YOU ARE FACING YOUR OWN DETOUR

1. Remain open-minded to a different solution.

2. Life is always working in your favour, so trust that everything is serving your highest good.

3. Just because something is not working to your timelines, that doesn't mean it's not happening.

4. If you are continuously adapting, you'll never fail – you'll simply change course.

Answered prayers often come in the form of delays and setbacks, making them difficult to recognise.

AMBER LYON — YOU ARE A MAGNET

Guiding principle

# Find Your Vision Holders

Part of the brain's process in breaking down a limiting belief is finding enough evidence to support a new belief. In fact, trying to create new beliefs *without* evidence often creates delusions, and delusions don't carry us very far.

You may still feel like the embodiment of your truest self is not possible or feel some resistance to it. In order to show yourself that this way of living is not only possible but completely within reach, you need to find evidence that it's possible – *you need to find your vision holders.*

Vision holders are people that already embody a trait, career, partner, physical state or confidence that you see in your magnetic self or authentically crave for your life. Intuitively, you'll have a gut feel as to who these people are, as you may already feel mesmerised by them or even, at times, envious. Envy or jealousy is just an indication that someone has something that you want, but that you don't quite believe it's possible for you. It's a signal that you need to find more evidence that this reality is within reach for you, too.

This is done by finding people you personally relate to or

can identify some similarities with so that you don't dismiss the possibility that the same magnetic state is possible for you, too. So often, we idolise people with whom we don't physically, culturally or financially have things in common, which leaves us feeling further away from what we want. It's the doomscrolling that leaves us feeling less than and miles away from the embodiment of our vision. The key is to find the success story of our visions, achieved by someone we can personally relate to. This process breaks through our disbelief with tangible evidence. And when we are creating new beliefs, we *have to see to believe*.

## ✳ FINDING YOUR VISION HOLDERS

1. Turn to social media or those around you. Who are you mesmerised by? Who already embodies the traits of your magnetic self? You can also think of movie characters or those in your wider circle. In the past, I've found great vision holders on YouTube also.

2. Write out a list of the ones who resonate with you the most.

3. These are your vision holders – the proof that what you are working towards is not only real, but achievable.

Envy or jealousy is just an
indication that someone has
something that you want,
but that you don't quite believe
it's possible for you.

AMBER LYON — YOU ARE A MAGNET

Guiding principle

# Scarcity vs Abundance Mindset

After living with my father for a period, my family was divided in two: my brothers lived in the city with my father, and my sisters and I moved to a small ski town in the South Island of New Zealand. The split was intended to keep my sisters and me somewhat protected from my father as he slid deeper and deeper into drug addiction. Mum supported us as best she could, working full time, juggling three girls at home and dealing with her own process of losing her husband to addiction.

Week to week, the budget was tight. Each time I'd join Mum going to the supermarket I'd be met with the same reminder: 'We don't have much left over for food this week, so we've got to be smart'. I'd run around the supermarket and pick up what I could for school lunches. She'd always be lighthearted about it, although even at such a young age I knew it wasn't how most families in the area went about their weekly shop.

Over time, I noticed something strange: even when she took up extra hours or worked to tighten the budget elsewhere, the supermarket story remained the same, each and every time. There was never any more (or any less) to meet our needs.

This was the first time I noticed how our belief system becomes a self-fulfilling prophecy. When we tell ourselves there won't be enough, there never is. When we tell ourselves there's just enough, there always is. And when we tell ourselves there's more than enough, there always will be. It is the narrative that we tell ourselves that our minds then seek to prove. Our minds are constantly seeking evidence to affirm the stories we tell ourselves, regardless of their truth or accuracy.

We usually associate the concepts of scarcity and abundance with money. But while they can apply to our finances, scarcity and abundance are, in fact, belief systems about the world. If we fundamentally believe that we live in a world with ample opportunity for success, connection and appreciation, that then becomes what we notice the most evidence for.

What we focus on in our environment essentially becomes the world we live in – because that is what we notice most on a day-to-day basis. The same can be said for those who believe that the world is a difficult place to live in, where there is not enough opportunity and a lack of great people to connect with. That then becomes *their* reality – because their minds seek to confirm what they believe.

A lot of the time we hold an abundant mindset in some areas of life, but a scarcity mindset in others. We can all think of someone who is financially successful but who cannot for the life of them find a safe and secure partnership; or someone who always seems to have a great relationship, but struggles to find clients for their business or to excel in their career.

Your own unique blueprint of belief and past experiences determines the areas in which you feel expanded and abundant, and where you do not. The following breakdown should help you to identify which mindset you may be currently

Our minds are constantly
seeking evidence to affirm
the stories we tell ourselves,
regardless of their truth
or accuracy.

AMBER LYON — YOU ARE A MAGNET

operating in – have a read and see if any of the points resonate with you.

# Abundant-mindset signals

- A deep inner knowing that there is more where *that* came from

- A sense of trust that something will happen, even if there is an absence of evidence right now

- Being inspired by others doing well (evidence that you can do it, too)

- A belief that there is enough space for everyone to do what they love and succeed at it

- Feeling there are many wonderful people you can't wait to connect with

- A belief that everything is working in your favour

- Believing that you can take care of yourself

- Not thinking that if one person succeeds, there is less space for you to do so

# Scarcity-mindset signals

- If someone else does well, that means there is less room for me to do so – there is not enough room for everyone to succeed

- Envy of others doing well (evidence that you can't do it)

- A belief that there's not a lot of opportunity in your career

- Telling yourself that there's not anyone out there that you connect with

- Judging others for spending habits

- Statements like 'It's really difficult to be successful at . . .'

- Belief that something is unrealistic

When we are in a scarcity mindset, two things happen: we prevent ourselves from seeing the many opportunities to connect, share, earn or create and we direct our energy towards confirming a scarce outcome (i.e. we unconsciously create situations that ensure we won't have enough – be it money, time or connection). This can look like wanting a loving relationship but actively avoiding situations where we could meet new people or spending more during periods when we earn more, putting us right back to where we started financially.

An abundance mindset is built on a sense of trust – a deep inner knowing that there is more where that came from. When we have an abundance mindset, we allocate our time, energy and attention towards finding opportunities or evidence for that reality. Our minds remain wide open. Suddenly, where we saw blocks, we see redirection to a new path. It opens up the possibilities of alternate solutions that scarcity does not allow for.

When seeking advice from anyone, it's important to acknowledge whether they are in an abundance- or scarcity-based mindset in the area in question. Advice is usually based on experience, so if someone experiences a scarce world, they will give you advice from this perspective. Similarly, if you speak to someone who has an abundance mindset, you'll receive advice from that perspective.

Just as we can be mindful of where others are coming from, you can be mindful of your own mindset by checking in with the lists on the previous pages regularly. You get to choose which world you live in: one that is overflowing with opportunities to feel good and be delighted or one that is not.

## ✻ CHANNELLING AN ABUNDANCE MINDSET

1. See to believe it's possible by finding vision holders (see page 212) for the area of your life you are looking to expand in.

2. When you find yourself making assumptions that reinforce scarcity, pause and ask yourself: how do I know this to be true? Can I find evidence for the contrary?

3. When you notice thoughts of scarcity pop up, ask yourself: where did I first learn this way of seeing the world? Is this *my* truth, or is it a truth I have absorbed from those around me growing up?

4. Each day, remind yourself of something that is abundant in your life. In doing so, you reinforce a new perspective.

Guiding principle

# It's All about Your Bounce-Back Rate

Arguing or resisting circumstances puts us into a state of misalignment. When we live in this place, we are on a different radio frequency to answers that could lead us to a better path. We simply can't hear solutions when we are focusing only on what's going – or has gone – wrong.

It may feel unnatural, but you've got to redirect your focus. Spending your energy focusing on what's happened (beyond reflecting on whether there's something you can do to improve things going forward) is counterproductive to your progress. As important as it is to take time to process a major setback or disappointment, success is dependent on your *bounce-back speed* – the turnaround time between getting knocked back and getting back up and walking towards your goals determines how likely it is that you will achieve the results you seek.

The extent of our frustration to any setback is dependent on how long *we resist what has already happened.*

When you have taken some time to process whatever setback you may have faced, allow yourself to shift your focus from 'my life is happening to me' to 'I am happening to my life'. By choosing this magnetic mindset shift, you empower yourself to take new action. Disappointments and setbacks are a natural part of any journey towards your goals, and they only mean that your goals are impossible if that's how you choose to interpret them. When you spend less time focused on what went wrong, and more on what you can do next, your growth will be exponential. It's not about avoiding failure but embracing it as part of the ride towards success.

 ## REFLECTIONS ON BOUNCING BACK

Align yourself with solutions by asking simple questions:

- How could this be working in my favour?

- Is there a new way of looking at this?

- What traits would I require to navigate this with more ease and grace?

It's not about avoiding failure
but embracing it as part of the
ride towards success.

Guiding principle

# Seven Ways You'll Know What Is Right for You

It's really easy to get caught up with what looks right on paper, but the decisions of your life should be rooted in what truly feels authentic in your bones and that holds synergy with your core values and self.

Whether it's a place, person or opportunity – you will have your own intuitive take on whether it's right for you or not. Try to lean into your inherent instincts, rather than relying on logical answers alone. When you get close to your true self, you always land on the most empowered answer.

Check in with the list on the next page whenever you face a crossroads in your life or need to make a big decision. I always gain a sense of deep connection to myself and my own truth when I refer to it.

# ✳ SEVEN WAYS YOU'LL KNOW SOMETHING IS RIGHT FOR YOU

1. It celebrates your authenticity.

2. It calls for you to bring forward the best of yourself.

3. Although you may not feel ready, something larger calls you forward.

4. It will more than likely frighten you to say yes.

5. It feels just on the cusp of your comfort zone.

6. You feel more like yourself when you engage with it.

7. It holds space for you to grow, rather than retract.

The choices you make today can create a new world tomorrow.

AMBER LYON — YOU ARE A MAGNET

Guiding principle

# Trust Your Timeline

We all face an influx of information and advice that tells us that we need to be five years ahead of where we are in our careers, or that there should be more in our savings accounts or we should be coupled up and settled down by now. This can leave us feeling rushed for things to unfold or to be someplace we are not.

This pressure to meet some self-imposed timeline can lead to you making contrived decisions. Perhaps forcing you to go out on dates because your friends are already settled down. Or not investing in a new career interest because it would put you back to change positions now. But feeling behind where you 'should' be is denying that your life is in divine order.

Because the details of your life and what you've been through are uniquely your own, it makes perfect sense that your timeline would be different to those of others around you. So measuring where you are, relative to where they are makes no sense because we do not all run the same race. In fact, the goal isn't to arrive as quickly as possible, but to enjoy and evolve on the way there. There's no prize in being the first to reach the finish line. Rushing through it all would mean rushing to your end. When you are aligned with yourself and what feels true, you can let go of the need for things to happen by a certain point – because they will find you when they are meant to.

# ✳ LOVING REMINDERS FOR WHEN YOU FEEL RUSHED

1. Life isn't as linear as you as may think – sometimes a succession of things that feel like they are going nowhere can end up connecting in miraculous ways.

2. Speed does not determine success.

3. It is your everyday choices and how you feel about them that determine the quality of your life.

Measuring where you are,
relative to where they are makes
no sense because we do not
all run the same race.

AMBER LYON — YOU ARE A MAGNET

Guiding principle

# Be Radically Honest with Yourself

There is a difference between choosing to focus on the light in your life and pretending there's no darkness at all. The true beauty of the human experience is that without the contrast of difficult times, we wouldn't be able to appreciate the good in quite the same way. If you resonate as someone that often skips over the more challenging emotions that come up, it is my invitation to you to acknowledge how you really feel about things – to address it before you choose to move past it.

Every emotion we feel is perfectly natural and valid – it's all a part of our experience. Negative emotions are just an indication that what we are experiencing is not in line with what we want to create. It shows us where we may need to adjust our direction or, at other times, where we may be perfectly on track but just processing a loss or disappointment.

Without pausing to really observe and understand why we may be feeling the way we do, we miss the opportunity to more deeply understand ourselves and learn what we need to do in order to alchemise the emotion. Every experience, situation and relationship constantly reflects back to us where we are invited to grow. So skipping over our difficult emotions means missing out on the crucial lessons that live in our uncomfortable emotions. It may at first feel strange to get honest and start acknowledging the difficult stuff, but it's essential.

Although it may seem easier to skip over the depth of your emotional experiences, in doing so you delay the lesson that has been so delicately placed in your life. In fact, our lessons tend to present themselves over and over again until we take the time to face them head on. Dancing over larger issues doesn't make them go away – it just delays our healing. It's not about swimming in them longer than we need to but sitting with them long enough to validate and soothe ourselves. We don't have to pretend we're ok when we're not. In fact, in doing so, we abandon our need for compassion and deny others the opportunity of supporting us during a difficult time.

It is our peace with our uncomfortable emotions that teaches our inner being that it is safe to feel. Although they may feel confronting to sit and be with — these feelings will pass. Emotions rarely stick when we sit with them, rather they begin to lift like mist on an early morning.

## ✳ SELF-HONESTY EXERCISE

1. Take out a pen and paper and, being radically honest with yourself, explore the following: how are you really feeling? Write for as long as it takes to let yourself get it all out, without any sugar coating.

The true beauty of the human experience is without the contrast of difficult times we wouldn't be able to appreciate the good in quite the same way.

2. When you are finished, place your hand on your heart and
   affirm: 'I accept myself for who I am and how I am feeling
   in this moment. I am here for you and everything is going
   to be ok.'

3. Next, write down three things you could do to support
   yourself (or ask from others in order to receive support).

Guiding principle

# Real Self-Worth Radiates from Within

It's hard to have faith that we deserve and are worthy of what we want before we have the proof in front of us. It can lead us to seek validation from others – as though they must believe we are worthy of what we want in order for it to happen. As if someone else's validation is the golden ticket that gives us permission to fulfil our potential in life. But we cannot wait for someone else to see our value before believing in ourselves – that relies too heavily on the ever-changing opinions of others.

Ultimately, you will never see your value clearly through someone else's eyes. And that's because your value is inherent. No relationship, experience or circumstance can change it, and when you try to measure it through others' eyes, you set your-self up on the rollercoaster of validation, tethering your sense of worth to how others perceive you. Then, in so doing, you become externally focused. Suddenly, your sense of self becomes entangled with the fickle thoughts and opinions of others: if they do not see you as worthy, it must mean that you are not.

Real self-worth comes from within. It's that quiet, still, knowing inside each of us that we do, in fact, deserve what we want. When we hold steady in that internal place, we reclaim the power we may have given away to others to dictate our worth. This radical self-acceptance magnetically radiates from within us, aligning us with what we desire because *we will no longer tolerate anything less.*

If you are doubting whether you can have what you desire, your higher self is calling for you to reinforce your deservingness through action. The more you show up for what you want, even with the doubt still present, the less potent the voice of uncertainty becomes. Eventually, doubt is no longer the barrier between you and the action you need to take. You'll come to see it as the veil that you must walk through to encounter your dreams.

The naysayers will always try to convince you that you are not enough for the world, but it is up to you whether you choose to believe them or not. And sometimes you are even your own naysayer. You've got to cultivate courage as you walk towards what you want because the world needs more people who are willing to be themselves. As you embody this, you teach others that they are capable of doing the same, giving them permission to follow *their* dreams, despite the criticism they may receive along the way. Ultimately, your capacity to fulfil your dreams and have what you want is inextricably tied to your capacity to believe in yourself. You were born inherently worthy and deserving of what you desire in life. Your desire alone is a signal of potential you are inspired to fulfil – a unique destination you are called to travel to. The experience of worthiness comes as a result of taking action, even when you do not feel worthy.

Be a role model for those around you:  trust yourself, stand

You've got to cultivate courage as you walk towards what you want because the world needs more people who are willing to be themselves.

AMBER LYON — YOU ARE A MAGNET

true in your inherent worth and let your own doubts and others' simply wash away like water.

## ✳ REMINDERS FOR CULTIVATING SELF-WORTH

1. The world needs more people who are courageous enough to be who they truly are.

2. When you show up in this authentic way, you inspire others to also own their true selves – magnetic energy is infectious.

3. Whether or not someone else thinks you are worthy of what you want is irrelevant – *unless you believe them.*

4. When you own who you are, you are naturally magnetic. Life begins to reflect back people, experiences and situations that are aligned with your worthiness.

Guiding principle

# Ask Yourself before You Ask the World

There have been many times in my life where I've found myself mentally exhausted from trying to figure out the best decision to make. I'll weigh the pros and cons of both and end up finding each case as strong as the other.

This process comes into play when I well and truly feel I don't have the answer. Therefore, the answer must exist outside of me, and so that's exactly where I try to find it – in the minds of those around me, whether trusted friends, family or those more experienced in the area in question.

These are generally great resources to draw on and can indeed help to point us in the right direction; but in using them, we also end up bypassing our own natural process of trusting that we are able to figure it out ourselves. Each of us has the ability to access our own deep truths. But as soon as we declare, 'I don't know,' or 'I don't have the answer,' that is exactly what we are going to experience.

A clever way to trick ourselves into tapping into our intuition is to ask: 'If I thought that I did know, what would my answer be?' or 'What would my truest self do in this situation?'

# Each of us has the ability to access our own deep truths.

Self-inquiry along these lines allows us to explore what it would look like if we did, in fact, know the answer. Maybe we wouldn't need to call a friend or spend so long trying to figure things out. Maybe the answers have been there all along, hiding beneath our belief that they are not.

I'm a big believer in reinforcing self-trust, and a huge part of trusting ourselves is being willing to sit with the discomfort of not knowing, in the knowledge that we are going to be fine figuring it out along the way. If we continuously seek out answers from the world around us before giving ourselves the chance to even attempt to answer, we deprive ourselves of the opportunity to listen to our own intuition.

It's natural to feel uncomfortable while you are trying to figure it out. You don't have to land on an answer straight away. And if you have something coming up, it's fine to share and ask for advice – but try to sit with it first, even if only for a moment, to see what your own answers would be.

## ☀ REINFORCING YOUR INNER GUIDE

1. Start by making micro-decisions – many small ones throughout the day. Once you've made a choice, trust that it was the best one and resist the temptation to question it.

2. Avoid seeking out advice from others until you've first asked yourself.

3. Ask yourself: which decision brings me closer to my highest self?

Guiding principle

# Treat Yourself Like Someone You Love

Growing up, my sister gave me a great piece of relationship advice: watch what people do, not what they say. This saved me from getting caught out by the pretty promising words of others if their actions didn't align. But only recently, I realised I was not applying this observation to the most important relationship of all – the one I have with myself.

I'd make myself little promises, like 'I'm going to work out tomorrow,' or 'I'm not going to do that anymore,' that didn't seem so significant if I let them slip. But over time, every promise I broke reinforced a deep mistrust in my own word. Here I was looking forensically into whether I could trust others when I clearly couldn't even trust myself.

The way we speak to ourselves matters, but what matters most is *how we treat ourselves*. It is our behaviour that reinforces what we believe to be true about ourselves and shapes our self-image. If someone else consistently went back on their word, and didn't follow through when they said they would,

Self-love is not an inherent trait. It is an accumulation of choices that support your wellbeing and acknowledge your worth.

AMBER LYON — YOU ARE A MAGNET

we'd certainly be prepared to sit down and have a conversation with them, putting a clear boundary in place. But what about sitting down and having a conversation with ourselves? Part of being magnetic is taking total responsibility for our actions by doing just that.

These conversations don't have to come from a place of blame or judgment, but rather from one of compassion and understanding. Check in and ask yourself why you may have been slipping on things you know to be important? What do you need to do in order to better support yourself? What rewards or consequences could you put in place to reinforce or break certain habits?

When you love someone, it's important to be able to sit down and tell them when they aren't acting in alignment with their potential. When they start to neglect your needs within the relationship, you've got to be able to communicate, rather than put your head in the sand and pretend nothing's wrong. And the same is true for the relationship you have with yourself.

Self-love is not an inherent trait. It is an accumulation of choices that support your wellbeing and acknowledge your worth. When you start to show up and treat yourself like someone you love, your whole being notices; your self-image, confidence and belief in your capacity exponentially expand because your actions show you that you are someone who follows through on their word. So when you say you are going to do something, *do it*. Even the small stuff – because how you do the small stuff determines how you see yourself.

# ✸ THE POWER OF FOLLOWING THROUGH ON LITTLE PROMISES

1. Every time you make a small promise to yourself and you fulfil that promise, you reinforce your belief in your own word and build self-trust.

2. It's not your words that determine your self-esteem, but how you treat yourself on a regular basis.

3. When you treat yourself like someone you love, you will radiate a new-found energy.

4. Get into the habit of asking: am I taking good care of myself? What could I do this weekend to nourish my mind, body or soul?

# ✳ TEN KEYS TO CHANNELLING A MAGNETIC MINDSET

1. Create time and space to connect with yourself and your inner guidance.
2. Carefully question any thoughts that dim your light.
3. Trust that you are always exactly where you are meant to be.
4. Listen to your gut feelings and act on them.
5. Show up before you feel ready, knowing that you'll gain the skills along the way.
6. Treat yourself with the same love and care you'd expect from others.
7. Stay open-minded to the way your life is unfolding.
8. Know that no change comes without an unseen gift.
9. Always ask yourself: what is this trying to teach me?
10. Take the time to appreciate the simple pleasures in your life.

PART FOUR

# Guiding Principles
# for Living in Joy

## Guiding principle

# You Never Know What Will Grow

New beginnings are never as obvious as they seem. A decision made in a moment to make better choices . . . writing out a business plan on a rough piece of paper . . . nervously catching someone's eye across a room . . . Each of these sparks something new, something unknown – the beginning of a new story that we could not possibly predict.

Like fertile soil, *this* moment is a place where we can plant the seeds of what we so deeply desire in life. We cannot know which seed will come to fruition, but we must plant them all nonetheless. We must tend to each with the same love, commitment and care as we would if we knew their growth was inevitable.

Sometimes, despite our love and effort, things don't grow to be what we would have liked – but sometimes they do. It's not our job to try to figure out what's going to grow and what will not. Our job is to stay open to pouring into our beginnings, even when we have been disappointed in the past.

When I first moved to New York from New Zealand it was quite a culture shock going from a community where I knew my neighbours and I could leave my car unlocked outside my house to living in the concrete jungle, where people often did or said whatever they had to in order to get ahead. One afternoon, particularly jaded after a disappointing day of castings, I sat down with my sister sharing that I had reached the point where I was struggling to trust new people and situations. She extended some loving guidance, reminding me that although there would be experiences in the city that would disappoint and make me question my vulnerability, to try and remain open. Even in the thick of it all, to do my best to stay in touch with the optimism and potential of every interaction and situation. Sure enough, the disappointing experiences did come, and in boatloads. But *anything worthwhile is absolutely worth risking disappointment for.* And one of our greatest challenges in life is to stay soft to what could be when it would be so much easier to harden.

If we are open to our futures being different to what we've experienced so far, the possibilities of the next moment are endless. Each new day brings a variety of moments that could be the start of something greater than anything we have ever experienced before. But the only way to know what could be is to give it a chance to show us. Just because we've been disappointed in the past, it does not mean we will have the same experience again, but one sure way to make that a reality is to not give it the chance to start with.

We must actively soften ourselves to our lives. Let go of our expectations of what will happen next and allow the experience to inform us. Let go of the idea that pouring love into something that does not work out how we would have liked is love wasted. Our love is never wasted; it's all part of a lesson on our way to where we are going next.

One day, when something grows better than you could have

Anything worthwhile
is absolutely worth risking
disappointment for.

imagined, you'll be so grateful that you remained open to what could be.

## ✳ REMINDERS FOR TENDING TO YOUR BEGINNINGS

1. No love is ever wasted. Give without expectation and allow each experience to inform you.

2. You cannot control which moment will flower into what you so authentically desire, so approach each one with the same positivity and effort. Remember to soften. Each moment is new and holds something new for you, a chance to grow.

Guiding principle

# Focus On One Thing at a Time

It's something that I've encountered time and time again: losing my momentum to start, before I've even begun. Struck by inspiration, or simply the need to complete a series of tasks to meet a goal, my mind begins to scatter. I leap ahead and wonder, how will step five lead to step six? And what about the fact that I don't even know how to do step seven? Then, what started out as inspired becomes entangled and downright confusing. With all the thoughts and mental gymnastics, it almost feels like I'm making progress, but at the end of the day, I find myself perfectly positioned at square one.

Focusing on the entirety of a task always feels daunting. Like a looming landscape casting a shadow upon you, your largest goals can feel like an insurmountable mission. When you look at the whole journey, it's easy to become discouraged to the point that you do not set out at all. With too much on your plate, even the simplest of tasks becomes overwhelming and your ability to effectively complete anything at all is diffused. But you would be astonished at what is possible when you take your focus from the whole and place it on each individual part. The smaller the part, the more achievable and realistic it becomes. In fact, with each step you take, you gain the exact skills required for the next. Then, what may have felt impossible before beginning, begins to feel like a natural progression, simply because you are *already in motion*.

You may not feel capable of hiking for six hours, but you can certainly take one step. And that one step can be followed by another and another. Soon, without nearly as much effort and stress, you find yourself atop the peak. Your goals then become the realisation of many small actions, rather than one enormous rush of energy.

## ✳ BREAKING DOWN THE VISION

1. You can apply this to your day-to-day life by prioritising your to-do list. Try ordering things by reflecting on which single task would make the most impact today. And then order each task down from there.

2. Be sure to acknowledge yourself once you've completed each task. It's important to celebrate the small wins throughout the day – they are the foundations for the big ones.

With too much on your plate, even the simplest of tasks becomes overwhelming and your ability to effectively complete anything at all is diffused.

Guiding principle

# Choose Flow over Force

How many times do you hold so tightly to what you want to happen that you end up resisting what is actually happening? How many days go to waste like this?

I've gone about most of my life with this playbook strategy, and as you can imagine, it didn't work out very well. Time and time again, I'd focus all my energy on forcing a certain outcome and end up disheartened or disappointed if life did not play along. I'd even start telling myself stories like 'This will never work,' just because things weren't happening according to my timelines or expectations.

Trying to control the world and what happens next is like trying to swim upstream against the flow – we exert a lot of energy and end up exactly where we started. And as much as we try, as much force as we apply, we cannot force the current to change. And who's to say that we should?

Although we can influence and prepare ourselves for a certain outcome, we can never know for sure exactly how something is going to unfold. In fact, most of the time, the way we'd like things to unfold is limited to what we believe is possible – but what about the realm beyond that? What if there was another outcome even greater than what we imagine for our lives?

Imposing expectations on to our lives deprives us of noticing all the miraculous ways it is trying to guide us towards new solutions and new experiences – ones that might take an alternate route that leads to what we so desperately crave. We might not be able to make sense of it all until we arrive where we always wanted to go. But what if we trusted where it led and remained open to what happened next?

When we accept what is happening in our lives, we open ourselves to seeing what's in front of us more clearly. Suddenly, we can look at our lives as an invitation to explore a new way forward and let ourselves be guided by the events that unfold, rather than impose our restrictions on what should. When we flow with the river of our lives, we will always arrive where we are meant to be.

The sooner we trust our lives are always unfolding in perfect order, the sooner we will be able to surrender the idea that our way is the only way. We can either flow with where our lives wants to lead us, or we can swim upstream. Which will you choose?

When we flow with
the river of our lives,
we will always arrive where
we are meant to be.

# ✳ REMINDERS FOR WHEN YOU ARE TRYING TO FORCE YOUR PLANS ON LIFE

1. How could you let go of your expectations? How could you more fully lean into trust that everything is unfolding as it should?

2. Flow outweighs force.

3. Remain open-minded to alternative ways of seeing the way forward.

4. Life is always working in your favour. If it does not make sense right now, it will in time.

## Guiding principle

# Peace Is a Choice

I always figured that a peaceful mind was a result of a peaceful life. But the truth is, life is never calm for very long. Day to day things pop up – little stressful moments that accumulate and slowly start to shift our moods. The little moments brew turmoil in the mind and create tension in the body.

Getting stuck in traffic; missing the train and running late are all perfect opportunities to throw you off balance. But you have an innate gift: the ability to choose how you feel, separate to what is happening around you.

Peace of mind is much less a state of being than a daily conscious choice: to face the invitation of stress and put peace of mind first; to observe the situation, accept it for what it is and come back to a place of inner calm. It's not about denying that things can be overwhelming or stressful but rather deciding that no matter the stress, how you feel in this moment is more important. So, for example, instead of becoming more and more infuriated while sitting stuck in traffic, perhaps you use the extra time as an opportunity to listen to an interesting podcast or your favourite playlist.

Life will always be sending a constant flow of personalised invitations to stress. It is up to you whether you wish to keep accepting.

Life will always be sending
a constant flow of personalised
invitations to stress. It is up
to you whether you wish
to keep accepting.

AMBER LYON — YOU ARE A MAGNET

# ✳ REFLECTION

The next time you find yourself stuck in traffic or agitated about how long something is taking – check in and ask yourself: do I want to feel this way? Does being stressed right now change the outcome? Can I let this tension go?

# Focus On What's Already Present in Your Life

It's natural to have strong desires for what we want in life: great friendships, full social lives, a loving relationship, expanding careers . . . the list goes on. Each desire we have is a divine right for us to enjoy and experience, but so often, when we obsessively focus on what it is we want, we end up hung up on what's missing from our lives, rather than what's already abundantly present and shining bright, right in front of our eyes.

If what we want is currently not present, it can end up seeming like we've been left behind or forgotten – like the feeling of the bus that never picked us up. It can start to feel like our sheer craving for something is a signal that it's out of reach, possible for others but somehow not for us. We become acutely aware of those around us who seem to effortlessly have what we desire so much. Our focus shifts into acknowledging all the shortfalls in our lives and we begin to embody a scarcity mindset. It's not that we are actively trying to make ourselves feel terrible, but it's impossible to sustain a great mood and appreciation for our lives when we are noticing everything that doesn't measure up.

If you're facing a great in between – the gap between what you have, and what you so honestly crave – please take solace. You are not alone. Nor are you flawed or unworthy. This time in your life is, as always, teaching you. It is shaping you into who you are here to be. There is always going to be a gap, and you've got to make peace with this truth and allow it to be a transition, rather than your destination. Because as soon as you have what you want, your desires will spring forth once again and create space between what you have and what you want. Think to yourself for a moment about something you have in your life now that you once so desperately craved. Isn't it fascinating that as soon as you attain it, your focus almost immediately jumps to what you'd like next?

This process is what keeps you moving forward and growing in your life. Although delays never feel great, they teach you a great deal about yourself. In the gap between what was and what will be, there you are.

When you shift your energy and attention back to what is in front of your two feet, you can start to see the little clues that lead you to what you desire. By showing up more fully now to what is already present in your life, you take the pressure off yourself to make it anything other than what it is. It won't be this way for ever – it never is. You will get to where you wish to go, but you have to be here now to get there.

You will get to where you wish to go, but you have to be here now to get there.

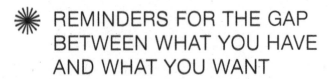

# REMINDERS FOR THE GAP BETWEEN WHAT YOU HAVE AND WHAT YOU WANT

1. Shift your focus from what's missing to what's abundantly present in your life.

2. Let go of the specifics. Allow life to surprise and delight you as to exactly how things will unfold.

3. Feeling the absence of what you want does not mean you are unworthy.

4. Trust that what you desire is already on its way to you.

5. Bring your attention to this present moment – to the fullness of your presence within it. When you are here, with this day, you will start to notice the clues that light you up and lead you to what you want.

Guiding principle

# Small Tweaks Can Lead To Massive Results

Consistency is one of the most powerful skills in attaining your goals, but consistency alone without considering results or measuring effectiveness might not be moving you forward. So if you're working towards a goal but it feels like nothing is flowing and there appears to be little to no progress, it might be time to change things up a little.

Your mind is a powerful creative problem solver; allow yourself to play with new ideas and to implement them accordingly – because small tweaks can completely change your trajectory. Tiny little pivots make it possible to test and trial different methods that may fast track your progress. It doesn't have to be a dramatic shift – just something that you might not have tried yet.

I remember a close friend of mine encouraging me to never stop playing with new ideas for my writing with no expectation of outcome, and as I allowed myself to evolve creatively, so did my writing and its reach.

It's important to take action and do what we can to move closer to what we want, but imposing restrictive timelines on achieving those things can blind us to what's actually working or not. Even when things *are* working, it pays to allow ourselves a little freedom to remain curious and adaptable. Could there be an even better solution to the problem at hand? Is there a new way of communicating that we may not have explored?

You cannot begin to imagine the extent of your mind's creativity once encouraged.

##  REFLECTION

Where in your life could you play with a new solution or approach? It may be an area where you feel things have become stagnant or just don't seem to be flowing, or perhaps one where you're thriving but have stopped exploring new ideas. I invite you to look at these areas of your life with a fresh perspective. Innovative ideas come from a place of playful curiosity (a judgment-free zone). Let go of what you think will or won't work and allow yourself to toy with different solutions. Grab a pen and paper and write out at least five alternative ways you could approach things.

You cannot begin
to imagine the extent of
your mind's creativity
once encouraged.

Guiding principle

# Flip the Coin

There is always another way of looking at things, although it may not seem like it. When we flip a coin and it lands on one side, it does not mean the other side does not exist – it's just that it is not visible to us. And life is much the same. We assume that what we see must be all there is. But what if there was another way of looking at it? A way of flipping the coin?

I'm not quite sure when I first realised that my mother was spiritual. As a child, you don't tend to categorise and label others quite so quickly. There were subtle clues in our home – spiritual books, tapes and auric visuals – but without anything to suggest otherwise, I assumed this was normal of all homes.

The biggest clue of all was my mother's demeanour – her capacity to handle challenge and pain and alchemise them into strength and joy. Through all the pain she experienced in life (the death of her parents, the emotional abuse from my father, the struggle of raising five children alone), she never wore it on her being for long. Somehow, in some way, she always managed to find the light and move forward.

Whether consciously or not, I learned my mother's way of interpreting the world; without it, I am not sure I would be sitting here typing these very words. In my darkest moments, caught in the depths of my mind, I knew I could call her and she would help me to find the light at the end of the tunnel (however distant it may have been). Then, in time, it became more and more natural for me to find the light myself.

I remember a specific night when I could not escape the sensation of impending doom. A blanket of meaninglessness seemed to cover my entire existence. For those who are reading these words and recognise themselves within them, I know that you too understand the pain of losing touch with the meaning of life: emotions feel void of depth, connections feel replaceable and existing itself begins to feel like an intolerable burden. There are many reasons why we can be hit by a wave of meaninglessness, but at times, there is no attributable source at all. It comes and it engulfs us, the weight of the wave sending us deep below the surface. On this particular occasion, feeling the weight on my chest and a tightness in my throat, I picked up the phone and dialled my mother, simultaneously hoping desperately that she would answer and that she would not.

As I sat quietly on the phone with her, she slowly questioned my thoughts with me. When I explained to her that everything seemed to be losing its meaning, she made the most simple, yet profound pronouncement: 'Life is meaningless, darling.'

The pure surprise of hearing her response shocked my system.

'But,' she went on, 'what is meaningless is equally meaningful. You get to decide which way you see it. It will always be both.'

I had not considered the reality of both truths. That when we feel the meaninglessness of life, we are not right or wrong, we are just focusing on one part of a greater story. The coin always has two sides. You get to decide how you see your life: will you consider its end and feel like your time is running out? Or will you consider yourself blessed for every moment given? You can see your work as a means to pay the bills or you can see it as a way to serve the world. You can see relationships as a tax on your time or as adding a true richness to every moment shared.

We live in a world of polarity, one that seems to tell us there is only one way to see things – that there is room for one truth and one truth alone. But this is not the case. At any given moment there are endless interpretations you can make about your life. And if what you find starts to feel like a burden, just flip the coin.

## ✳ THREE LOVING REMINDERS

1. There is always another way of seeing your life.

2. Someone else is praying for what you have come to take for granted.

3. There is mundanity and enormous beauty in most things you do – you get to choose which side you focus on.

You get to
decide how you
see your life.

Guiding principle

# Reconnect with Your Sense of Awe

When you begin to scratch the surface of what we've uncovered about the universe, it's difficult to comprehend just how magic it all really is. This state of being – in awe of life – reflects how we see the world as children. Before the world told you what everything is, you wondered as a child how it came to be. When we label something, we take away the vast complexity of it. The trees that were once magnificent worlds to climb became just a word – trees.

We lose touch with the magic of life when we place things in clearly defined boxes. But living in awe is such a beautiful magnetic energy to occupy. It's open-minded, curious, delighted and in tune with the true beauty of life. When we pause and consider what we may have come to gloss over, we reconnect with the magic of our world.

When we pause and consider
what we may have come
to gloss over, we reconnect
with the magic of our world.

#  RECONNECTING WITH AWE

1. On your morning stroll to work, or to grab coffee, take a moment to really observe the happenings of the world around you. Without headphones, your phone or anything else to distract you, see if you can notice something that you wouldn't ordinarily see. Can you try to see the world around you with a new found sense of wonder and curiosity?

2. You are representative of an unbroken lineage of life going back 4 billion years – all the way to the first single-cell organism.

3. There are more stars in the universe than the total of grains of sand on planet Earth.

# Each Moment Is Worthy of Delight

We've each been sold a misleading ideal: that feeling good about our lives happens once everything 'comes together', that there is a specific set of circumstances will allow us to finally sit back and say, '*Now, this is worthy of delight.*'

Each of us has a different measure for what that set of circumstances might be. For you it might be starting a family, buying a home or a specific career achievement. The truth is, however, that although rewarding, these achievements do not hold some magic capacity to deliver any more joy than the simple everyday pleasures of life.

In fact, each moment is equally as full and worthy of delight as the next. The first sip of your morning coffee, closing your eyes and turning your face towards the warmth of the sun, a cheeky look before bursting into laughter with a friend. These are the small moments that contain the true joy of being alive. And the sooner we learn to appreciate them, the greater the happiness we can experience each day, rather than outsourcing our delight to some future achievement.

Don't allow yourself to be fooled by your mind's future

promises of 'feeling good'. Choose to feel good now. Choose *you* now. Choose to find appreciation for the little moments of joy in your life that are already there waiting to be celebrated. The achievements will always be great signposts along the way, but they do not define your life, unless you let them. You cannot bottle a lightning strike, but you can witness the fragments of light in your life each day.

## ✳ BUILDING IN MOMENTS OF DELIGHT

1. Take a few extra moments to really appreciate a warm drink in the morning.

2. Send a message to someone you love, letting them know something you value about them.

3. When you are out and about, put your phone in your pocket and take the time to look for moments of joy around you (perhaps you'll see a child laughing or pass an elderly couple holding hands).

Choose to find appreciation for the little moments of joy in your life that are already there waiting to be celebrated.

AMBER LYON — YOU ARE A MAGNET

## Guiding principle

# Let Yourself Feel It All

To look at the world and to see all its beauty is simultaneously magnificent and terrifying. Because when we admit just how magic it all is, it's impossible not to acknowledge how afraid we are of losing it. When we let ourselves fully embrace how precious every little moment with those we love is, it becomes harder to let them go when it's time for them to leave. When we recognise that the nature of life is to change, it forces us to realise just how much we want things to remain the same.

To see the beauty of our lives is to be deeply vulnerable. But I'd rather live in the depth of it all and experience the rich tapestry of highs and lows than not let myself feel it at all.

The beauty of your life reminds you of how fleeting every moment really is; if you don't stop to look, you may just end up missing some of your most precious ones. Instead of rushing out the door to work, maybe you'd take in the look in your mother's or lover's eyes a moment longer. Perhaps you'd give them the grace of your full attention, rather than letting your thoughts race ahead into the day. Maybe you'd take a longer

When we recognise that the
nature of life is to change,
it forces us to realise just
how much we want things
to remain the same.

AMBER LYON — YOU ARE A MAGNET

drive home just to catch the evening light and watch how it paints the evening sky.

I know it's terrifying – but let it in. Let yourself acknowledge just how much things mean to you. When all is said and done, you'll look back and be grateful that you did, even if it made it more painful to see things change. Because the pain of change is the reward for being devoted to your life. To love and let go. And although you may not think so right now, you'll come to feel that way again.

Stay soft. Stay open. Let it in.

## ❋ THREE LOVING REMINDERS

1. You will never be able to repeat this moment once it has passed.

2. Although it's scary to sit with just how impermanent things are, it's not as scary as letting them pass you by without taking the time to fully appreciate them as they are.

3. If you take the time to notice, life will show you as much beauty as you choose to see.

# Choose to See the Light in Others

Every day, in every interaction and experience, you are invited to make an important decision: what energy will you contribute?

We are all presented with countless opportunities throughout the day to extend a little extra grace, patience and love where we may not be required to. Yet I encourage you to choose to do so. Choosing to be kind is not a reflexive response, but one that is cultivated with time, care and patience. It's not always the easiest choice. In fact, more often than not it requires diving deep into ourselves to not snap, yell or pick a fight when something doesn't go to plan. There are many easy invitations to judge strangers, condemning them for minor mistakes or delays, making endless assumptions on the type of person they are and just how different they are to us. But what if that was someone we loved? Would we behave differently? Would we extend them a little extra kindness and grace?

Choosing to see the light in others requires us to let go of the idea that the world is divided between us and them (us being the people we know, love and care for and them being everyone else). Every person we meet or cross paths with has

Choosing to see the light in others requires us to let go of the idea that the world is divided between us and them.

their own entire world unfolding before them. We can never imagine the complexity of a stranger's life – what they may or may not be struggling with or going through. Just as we would appreciate someone being kind to one of our loved ones if they were having a bad day, how can we too give that gift to someone else's mother, daughter, son or husband?

Kindness has a ripple effect on the world. In just one positive interaction – smiling, saying hello or wishing someone well – we can make an enormous impact on someone else's day. Shockingly, there are many stories of those who were planning to end their own lives abandoning their plan after a stranger asked them how their day was going. Can you fathom that for a moment? That just one simple gesture of kindness can be the difference between life and death. It's important to look after our own world and the people we love, but it is equally as important to extend compassion and kindness to those we do not know. Perhaps they need it most.

I have a simple invitation: try to spot the light in everyone you cross paths with today, even if it proves to be difficult. When you are tempted to judge, shut down or close off, see if you can find the light. You might just surprise yourself with what you notice. Everyone's light looks a little different. It may be the way they laugh, the softness of their eyes, a similarity they share with someone you love. When you let yourself see strangers as the lovers, brothers, mothers, sisters and sons of others, it helps you to remember that we really aren't so different. And your kindness is an incredible contribution to their day.

 SEEING THE LIGHT IN OTHERS

1. Bring to mind someone you love. Take a few moments to reflect on all of the qualities and traits you respect or admire about them.

2. Now bring to mind someone you find difficulty getting along with. Take some time to reflect on some or a single quality about this individual that you respect or admire. It may take longer, but keep searching until you find one.

3. Finally, bring to mind someone you feel neutral about (perhaps the person who works at a store you frequent, the barista at your local coffee shop or someone at your office). Take a few moments to consider something that you appreciate or admire about them.

Guiding principle

# Don't Wait – There May Not Be Another Moment

It's a strange thought to consider your own end. It remains one of the single truths and certainties we all share – something that binds us all together in our experience: that it begins and it will end (as we know it).

For most of my life, I hadn't really considered the idea of life ending. Perhaps, in part, because I was immersed in so many beginnings. Our early lives are all about how things are beginning to grow. A constant question looming in our minds: *'What's next?'*

Youth glows with a sense of indestructibility. Sickness and death are reserved for the elderly and exist someplace else other than our own homes. But what happens then, when we inevitably encounter the loss that comes early or is unexpected? Our lives enter the freefall of shock.

I was twenty-five when my father passed. It was in the midst of the time my boyfriend and I had taken off to travel together – in love and enjoying the greatest adventure of our

When you look at your life and the people within it through the eyes of impermanence, you give yourself a glimpse of just how meaningful they really are.

AMBER LYON — YOU ARE A MAGNET

lives. Untouchable. We had just arrived in Amsterdam late the night before and I remember the feeling of him lightly waking me, as I lay wrapped up in the hotel sheets. As I stirred, he let me know I had missed a few calls from my mother and that it might be a good idea to check what was going on.

As I called her back, a strange feeling began to sit in my stomach. Call it instinct or intuition, but my body was preparing me for the words that she would speak. He was passing, she explained – they were about to take him off life support and she asked if I wanted to say anything before he slipped away.

A brief gap between moments. No time to think. Only one chance to say the words that I had held hostage my whole life. She let me know that she was about to hold the phone to his ear and I let the words speak through me.

'I love you. I forgive you. I'd choose you again.'

And then the moments came together again and all I remember is the rise and fall of my chest with each stifled inhale and exhale and the tears pooling on Jon's arm. I was flooded by the release of twenty-five years of emotion and the shock of such a sudden goodbye.

My mother later told me how he had asked her to pass on just how proud he was and that he was sorry. A word I had never heard escape his lips. An admission passed on that I had so craved hearing myself.

I share this story not to frighten you that you may lose someone you love, but to better prepare you for when you do. Because the people in our lives are not as untouchable as we may have come to believe. They are precious and they are impermanent – just as is everything else in life. The sooner we accept this difficult truth, the sooner we can let go of the idea that there's time to make amends. That we can skip the family dinner because there's another one next week. That there will be a better time to speak the words we hold so fiercely in our hearts.

When you look at your life and the people within it through the eyes of impermanence, you give yourself a glimpse of just how meaningful they really are. It may feel foreign or strange but see if you can allow yourself the opportunity now to consider the impermanence of life – your own and those of others around you. Allow the emotion to swell in your body. This is the beauty of life – to love so deeply that it frightens you. We desire things to remain the same so much so that we deny a fundamental truth of life: that they were always destined to change.

Speak the words in your heart, not someday when – but now. Pick up the phone and have the conversation you've been saving for when there's a better time.

## ✳ FOUR LOVING REMINDERS

1. If you feel something, say it. We rarely regret what we did say more than whatever we didn't.

2. The idea that there's always more time is true – until the day that it is not.

3. Tell the people you care about how much you love them regularly.

4. Don't wait for birthdays or holidays to come together with friends and family; make it a part of your regular calendar. If you prioritise quality time together, you'll thank yourself later.

Guiding principle

# Just Be

What a glorious morning it is today. I've been sipping a warm drink, watching the first golden light creep through the trees, listening to the birds waking up and observing the colours of the day change between the minutes.

In these peaceful moments, I am reminded that the day does not perform – it simply is. The day does not put on an extra special show because I or anyone else is watching closely – it simply is. The day does not concern itself with striving to be the best that's ever been – *it simply is.*

I want to remind you today of this notion. Are there certain parts of yourself that you will show because someone is (or is not) watching? Do you shine brighter or more dimly based on who walks through your life? Do you put pressure on yourself to be a certain way, even though it may not feel true to how you really feel?

Today, I invite you to be all of who you are, with all that includes; every little trait – what you see as the good and the bad. Let go of the notion that you should adapt yourself to the circumstances or people you find yourself around. Let yourself be free to shine in whatever way feels most true to you.

Sometimes that will naturally mean you will not feel like shining at all – and that is ok; after all, it is the cloudy, grey days

Let yourself be free
to shine in whatever way
feels most true to you.

AMBER LYON — YOU ARE A MAGNET

that make us appreciate the sunshine all the more. But even on the days you might not have a bright and sunny disposition, you can still be utterly magnetic. Because when you own the truth of how you really feel in any given moment, you give yourself permission to be who you are. And when you are wholeheartedly yourself, you are captivating, no matter whether you feel like shining or not.

## 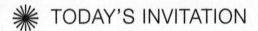 TODAY'S INVITATION

Be like the day: release the judgment, expectations and pressure to be anything other than what you are. You will rise and you will fall, you will shine and you will pour and, when all is said and done, you'll realise there was never any requirement for anything other than to simply be. Allow yourself to just be and feel whatever feels most truthful to you in this moment.

Guiding principle

# Say Yes to Your Life

There is a beautiful quote from the Soto Zen monk and teacher Shunryu Suzuki: 'Leave your front door and back door open. Let thoughts come and go. Just don't serve them tea.'[1]

Not serving our thoughts tea refers to the act of allowing and surrendering – letting things be as they are and not giving them more meaning than they have or coming up with elaborate stories as to why things happened the way they did.

Total freedom is accepting what is at every moment. Resisting what is happening because it is not unfolding according to your idea or plan is like holding yourself hostage, preventing yourself from enjoying your life as it is. If you find yourself in an experience that you no longer want to be in, thank this moment for allowing you to see that so clearly. Then, instead of resisting, you can channel your energy into creating meaningful change. The very act of accepting allows you to let go of the tension of the mind that's so wholly focused on resisting what is. As soon as you release that resistance, you open yourself to receiving

[1] As quoted in *Crooked Cucumber* by David Chadwick, 2000.

a new perspective on the situation so that you are left feeling empowered and evolved.

It's a three-part journey:

1. Accept

2. Release

3. Receive

What if we could let go of the need to compare what is right now to our ideas of what should or could have been? What if we let go of our ideas of what should happen and just say yes to what is?

Try it now. See how it feels in your body when you let go of your resistance.

## ✸ SAYING YES TO YOUR LIFE

1. New experiences are invitations life has sent for you to grow and evolve in the exact ways required for your next chapter.

2. You can practise the art of acceptance today by saying yes to every situation you find yourself in. Once you have accepted what is, you can make a new choice if you desire change.

Saying yes is not about celebrating what is happening, but simply releasing our resistance to its presence.

AMBER LYON — YOU ARE A MAGNET

Guiding principle

# Every Season Comes With Its Own Lesson

When things inevitably slow down in our lives, it's natural to feel frustrated and impatient. We are conditioned to measure our progress purely on external shifts. If things are not moving outside of us, how will we know how far we've come?

I have always been uncomfortable with rest. I've resisted any time in my life when things weren't moving forward at a pace that felt to me like meaningful progress. But each season of our lives brings about the exact climate for our growth.

It's in our winter season that we are given the time and space to turn within – to work on our internal worlds, to build our inner reservoirs, so that we have the skills and tools necessary for the next stage in our journeys. It may not make sense at the time, but this is because it is only seen clearly when we look back and can see how perfectly it fits into the story of our lives. In fact, denying ourselves this opportunity, and trying to force our lives to speed up, deprives us of the space we need to rest, recharge and prepare, so that we have the energy we need for the spring, when things will inevitably be busy once again. Because no season lasts for ever.

So when things slow down, lean into your self-care practices. Give yourself opportunities for introspection and indulge in restorative rituals. You can measure progress through simply acknowledging how you handle difficult situations differently, or noticing the kind words you speak towards yourself.

When things start to thaw, you'll have a reservoir of ideas and inspiration ready to plant for spring. Instead of trying to leap into summer, see if you can appreciate the gradual increase in tempo, taking your time to set up a strong foundation of habits. Then, when summer arrives, embrace it. When things start to speed up, lean into your life, say yes to opportunities that come your way and know that you can pause when you need to. And when autumn comes, as it always does, don't fret – just take the time to reflect on what you've learned and how you've grown through action.

Let each season of your life inform you. Instead of resisting or trying to skip ahead, trust that there is a lesson within this time for you.

## ✳ REFLECTIONS

1. What is the season of your life inviting you to do right now?

2. How could you lean into whichever season you are in more wholeheartedly?

3. What do you need to give yourself to have more patience for what is unfolding?

Instead of resisting or trying
to skip ahead, trust that there is a
lesson within this time for you.

Guiding principle

# Becoming a Magnet for Joy

External achievements do not change internal circumstances. I used to work as hard and as long as I could at attaining the outward goals that I thought would leave me feeling full and happy, but time and time again I'd be left with the same lingering hollowness. There I'd be, sitting and waiting for some magic wand of delight to be waved upon my mind, and a confident, cool, calm, collected self emerging on the other side. Yet no achievement was grand enough to change the way I felt about myself and my life.

As much as we try, changing our circumstances never truly changes what is happening within us. Although some temporary relief can come alongside a new haircut, a period of travel or rearrangement of the living room – wherever we go, there we are. We cannot escape the internal journey that our inner being begs for us to embark upon. External shifts without internal reflection become surface-level changes, like paint over wallpaper – what appears different is just the same wall in a new shade.

Getting out of the perpetual race towards a future of happiness and instead embodying joy in daily life requires redefining what joy means to you. Instead of placing your attention on what needs to externally change for you to feel good, you must bring your attention to the internal barriers that keep you from being a natural magnet for joy. In fact, when you seek out external achievements in an attempt to change your internal state, you all too often are met with the disillusionment that comes along with the fulfilment of shiny goals.

I now define joy as an internal state of being, rather than some externally triggered experience; not a moment, but an experience. Living in joy is living a life that feels good to you now, not someday in the future. Joy is our natural state of being. The effortlessness of a child's laughter. The art of noticing the world around you and the magic woven into each of its moments.

A joyful life is the result of the moment-to-moment choices each of us gets to make: to see the good, or to see the bad. A capacity and willingness to witness what's present in our lives, more than we notice what's missing on the way to our higher goals. This decision is in our hands.

Focusing on the good doesn't mean accepting a dissatisfying relationship or career because it's 'better than nothing'. It's not about fooling yourself. Rather, it's about finding the most empowering way to move forward, letting yourself be guided by hope, instead of fear.

Noticing the good leads to situations, experiences and people that align with your new magnetic energy, whereas when you constantly focus on what's missing, that places you in a state of lack, where you end up feeling you are running late for your own life.

I know that it sounds too simple, too straightforward to be true. That we need a new job, a new relationship or more money to finally meet our unique requirements of feeling good.

Happiness is not circumstantial, but a result of being able to *notice the things that bring you joy.*

AMBER LYON — YOU ARE A MAGNET

But how we feel is a result of what information we are attuned to notice most. Happiness is not circumstantial, but a result of being able to *notice the things that bring you joy*.

What are you waiting for in order to feel good about your life? What if right now – *as things are* – was enough for you to feel good about your path, knowing that things will continue to evolve and grow?

It's so important for your sense of progress and self-esteem to work towards goals and a life vision. But tapping into your most magnetic self isn't about idealising a future state, but using your vision as a framework for how you can show up as that self *today*. And in so doing, you bring your energy back into the present moment – the only place you can ever really change. When you allow the achievement of goals alone to define your sense of contentment, you set yourself up for a rollercoaster of emotions for the inevitable twists and turns life throws your way.

You are infinitely powerful, deserving of joy, love and abundance beyond your wildest imagination. An excess of delight stands before you, waiting for you to acknowledge it whenever you are ready.

I'll let you in on a little secret: no future moment is responsible for changing how you feel about yourself or your circumstances. Even the grandest of achievements or milestones are as fleeting in nature as a deep breath of fresh air on a cold morning. The enjoyment of your life lives in this present moment and in your ability to choose what you focus on. *This is a magnetic mindset.* Knowing that you are the one responsible for what you focus on most.

Every time you take your attention and place it upon what feels good to you, you align yourself with a state of joy. In this state, you magnetically pull towards you more information, experiences and people that radiate that same energetic state. Suddenly, joy is no longer reserved as an outcome, but becomes a state of being. A decision to feel whole from within, rather than seeking to fill the world without.

A good life is not someday when, it is chosen in every moment.

More love, opportunity and delight than you could possibly imagine are waiting for you, but it's up to you to claim this life. To choose to see where the love quietly sits in your life, even where you would not ordinarily go looking for it. When you attune your eye to see the light, the world will begin to glow for you, and you yourself will radiate that same magnetic energy into the world.

 ## AFFIRMATION

'I am a magnet for joy. When I focus on the good, the good gets better. I radiate this energy into every room that I enter.'

**Redefining what a good life is to you**

What does your life look like today? What tiny micro-moments of joy would you notice if you allowed yourself to see them? When you take down the pedestal you've created for what should be, or could be, what might you see in front of you? What if there was already enough evidence to feel good about yourself and your life?

# Afterword

And here you are, at the end of the book – a journey to move closer to yourself, amplifying the light that radiates so brightly within you. I hope that in these pages you have discovered more of yourself – more of the light that so abundantly exists within you and around you. When you tune into this state of being, you are naturally magnetic. In tune with all of the good in your world and within yourself. Try to remember not to get caught in the promises of 'one day when . . .' and to always bring your attention back to the present moment – *this is where your power lives*. When you set your vision, remind yourself that it's not about what you're trying to achieve so much as who you are being called to become that is truly important to your self-development. Most of all, try to enjoy it as much as you can.

Thank you for being here, and for embarking on this magnetic journey with me.

All my love.

Amber

# Acknowledgments

Nothing would be made possible without the support and guidance of those around me. I'd like to thank my mother for showing me what it means to truly live in joy and for being a living embodiment of love. My sister Alexandra for her wise words on long, late nights. Lauren, the best editor I could have asked for, along with your motivating belief and endless encouragement. And Jon, for being my rock and biggest supporter in bringing this to life.